PRAISE FOR

CARING FOR YOUR AGING PARENTS WHILE CARING FOR YOURSELF

As a professor of health and gerontology for the past 35 years, I have read numerous books related to caregiving—without a doubt, *Care-Grieve-Grow*, ranks at the top! Written from Fazio's personal experience and supplemented by years of owning a caregiving business, she provides essential step-by-step tools and resources vital for caregivers. Beautifully written, Fazio also weaves a blend of inspirational vignettes of the hardships, challenges and gifts of caregiving.

— C. Jessie Jones, Professor and Chair, Department of Health Science, California State University, Fullerton

"Care, Grieve, Grow" is a must read for everyone who is caring or will be caring for an aging parent. Karen opens up her heart retelling her own true story of help, guilt, sorrow, pain and joy in caring for her parents, preparing for their deaths and dealing with her own personal issues. Her story, practical advice and helpful tips have been invaluable to me as I face the same challenges in caring for my elderly mother. Her book constantly brings me solicit when I feel overwhelmed. Thank you Karen for your book truly helps with caring for our aging parents and for caring for ourselves in the process.

— Lisa Prats, BOMA International

"It is wise to gain knowledge and wisdom from those who have traveled the road before you, and that is exactly what Karen Fazio has offered in *Care, Grieve, Grow*. Written in a personal and compassionate manner, she offers valuable information, resources and experience on many sensitive topics with one's aging parents, as well as insights on how we, the children, can best deal with these issues. Ms. Fazio understands the many emotions and challenges for those suddenly in a care-giving mode and the reader will find solutions and comfort in these pages."

— Julie Hall, The Estate Lady

Care-Grieve-Grow goes beyond issues of care-giving and tackles the challenges of aging in our complex society. Everyone at some point will be impacted by many if not most of the topics in this book. Karen Fazio's journey is our journey and her book Care-Grieve-Grow is a powerful and relevant guide as we explore our aging journey.

— Jacquelyn Lauder, MSG Scan Health Plan

Karen offers a practical, compassionate, and essential guide for anyone navigating the caregiving experience. Care, Grieve, Grow instills hope that taking care of a loved one can be a rich and rewarding journey that ultimately brings us closer to ourselves.

— NATE MORRISSEY, BLUE SKY ESTATE SERVICES

"Care-Grieve-Grow is a heartwarming story told first person of how care giving opens up the relationship and dialogue between family members and how important emotional healing is to aging America as much or more than the physical care and support of family members. Karen serves as the guide using personal experiences, offering the reader powerful tools of empowerment and personal growth while detailing important information that every caregiver should know of.

— GEORGE STRICKLAND, PRESIDENT RIGHT AT HOME, CENTRAL ORANGE COUNTY

"This is an engaging book and a valuable resource for adult children of aging parents. Karen Fazio exhibits not only the knowledge of a true professional and wisdom of experience, but more importantly a depth of understanding, insight and compassion that comes from a heart that has been tempered by her own personal challenges. This book will help families to become better informed and prepared to make prudent, informed decisions when it is time to help their aging loved ones. It will also help them to understand and navigate the emotional challenges and stresses of caregiving.

— LINDA ARMAS, CSA, CERTIFIED SENIOR ADVISOR (CSA),
PRESIDENT CLEAR CHOICE SENIOR SERVICES

Karen provides a thoughtful analysis on caregiving through her own life lessons. She delivers alternative modalities that complement our traditional. Her interpretive writing style guides you to discover that the journey can lead to rewarding new relationships and personal self discoveries.

— MARILYN FEDOROW, COUNCIL ON AGING, ORANGE COUNTY

Care~ Grieve~ Grow

Caring For Your Aging Parents While Caring For Yourself

KAREN FAZIO MSG

ISBN: 0615842712
ISBN-13: 9780615842714
Library of Congress Control Number: 2013912190
Karen J Fazio, Huntington Beach, CA

CONTENTS

INTRODUCTION. xiii

1. One Hot, July Day My Life Changed Forever 1

   Realizing Your Parents Need Help. 3

   Where Do I Begin? Assessing Your Parent's Needs And Desires . . 4

   Activities Of Daily Living (ADL's). 5

   Where Will My Parents Live? 5

   Is My Parent's Home Safe?. 6

   Is Driving Safe?. 6

   Declining Health. 7

   Hearing And Eyesight 7

   Do You Suspect Dementia? 7

   Depression 9

   What Can You Do?. 10

2. Remember To Listen 15

   Planning For Care. 17

   Important Documents 17

   Estate Planning. 17

   Difficult Conversations 21

   People And Situations - *Ron, His Daughter And The Car Keys* . . .24

   What If My Parent Won't Stop Driving? 26

   Geriatric Care Manager. 27

   Summary 27

3. The Love And The Pain 31
     My Daughter, My Caregiver 32

4. Roles Emerge 37
     Family Dynamics 40
     Significant Relationships Count 42
     I'm An Only Child 43
     Resistance To Assistance 43
     Coping With Dementia 45
     When A Family Member Is LGBT 46
     My Mom Didn't Take Care Of Me, Why Should
     I Take Care Of Her? 47
     Show Me The Money 48
     Mental Illness 49
     Family Conflict 50
     Communication 51

5. Home Sweet Home 53
     Aging In Place 55
     Hiring A Formal Caregiver: Choosing The Right One 55
     Medication Management 60
     Home Modification And Monitoring 60
     Adult Day Care 62

6. Caregiver Stress And Burnout 65
     Asleep On My Feet 67
     Understanding Stress 69
     Physical Signs Of Stress 70
     Emotional Signs Of Stress 70
     What Can You Do? 72
     Are You A Control Freak? Be Honest 72

Caregiving And Co-Dependence. 73
Caregiver's Bill Of Rights 75
Tools For Survival 75

7. The Art Of Zen Caregiving 79
Touch Matters. 80
Holistic Care For You And Your Parent. 81
Complementary And Alternative Medicine (Cam) 81
Taking Care Of Your Body, Mind, And Spirit 86

8. When Is It Time For Placement? 97
How Do You Know It's Time?. 98
Safety 99
What Kind Of Environment Is Best For My Parent? 99
Living Options 99
Using A Placement Specialist. 104
Elderlaw Specialist. 105
The Emotions Of Placement 105
An Ombudsman Is Your Resource. 106

9. Fear And Love. 109
End Of Life. 111
End Of Life Wishes. 111
Palliative Care And Hospice .111
Religion And Spirituality. 114
End Of Life Gifts 116
Terminal Restlessness Or Agitation 118
After Death. 120
The Importance Of A Funeral Or Ceremony. 121
Your Parent's Belongings 123

10. Growth And Liberation 127
    "What You Feel You Can Heal" 132
    Stages Of Grief 132
    Grief Is Personal 135
    Who Am I Now? 135
    I Feel Like An Orphan 136
    Support Groups 137
    Other Groups And Classes .137
    Reading 137
    Explore Your Relationship .137
    Normal And Abnormal Grief 138
    Holidays, Birthdays, And Anniversaries 139
    A New Normal 139

Afterword 141
    A New Understanding 141

Resources 145

Recommended Reading 149

Index 153

To Mom and Dad –
*For the journey we traveled together; you **are** eternally cherished.*

ACKNOWLEDGMENTS

We all possess sacred stories that lie within us. Experiences that have shaped our lives, influenced our decisions, and ultimately become a part of the tapestry of what makes us who we are. I have learned time and time again that the challenges in life are truly what teaches us the most. It is through our efforts to overcome that we are offered the profound opportunity to dig deep so we may continually discover the treasures of truth that lie hidden within us. It is the relationships we form; those we meet along the way, animal and human, that join us on our personal stage of life; influencing our stories, touching and torching our hearts, seemingly giving and taking away – that we cannot do without. So many fellow travelers have beautifully decorated the stage of my life. For this, I offer you an ocean full of gratitude.

"Brother Rob," I believe it is only you and I who can truly understand the laughter and the tears; the paradox of each other's story and perspective on *those years*. Thank you for your friendship, love, and support. Beloved Brenna, I thank you . . . from the depth of my heart for embracing who I am and accompanying me on this cherished journey. You opened your heart and home to my mom before it crossed my mind. Thank you for the sacrifices you made - for me and my family. My deepest gratitude goes out to my "bestie," Cheri for always being my cheerleader. You believed in me when I did not – you are always there to support my various causes – even the *questionable* ones. We have laughed, we have cried, and we understand. Thank you for those long days and nights at the bedsides of my parents – your laughter eased the way. Debbie, you have been there when it counts. You never judged the shortcomings of my family, but instead offered them love and grace. Thank you for accompanying my dad to the doctor when I didn't think I could possibly bear another appointment filled with bad news. Thank you too, for showing up - unannounced to go for that run and eat that burrito with me – you made a difference – you brightened a very dark day. Thank you Jessie – you believed in me when I was a child and celebrate me as a woman – this means the world to me – without you, the journey would have been different.

I would also like to acknowledge all of the *players* on my stage – my family, my friends – who continually push me forward by accepting who I am and who I may become. All of you touch my heart, inspire me, and cause me to grow. Thank you to my feline allies, Baxter and Gypsy, for loyally holding the space around me during long hours at the computer. You are there, present in the now – always teaching me how to love even more. To every "older adult" who has crossed my path, personally or professionally, and taught me about surrender, vulnerability, wisdom, reflection, and letting go; thank you.

"The best classroom in the world is at the feet of an elderly person."

ANDY ROONEY

INTRODUCTION

If you are caring for aging parents in declining health, chances are you are overwhelmed with thoughts of how you will get through this difficult time. "Caring, grieving and growing" is not a linear experience to be sure. It happens all at once and contains within it various aspects of life. Caring for our aging parents is about much more than "caring for our aging parents." It's about us, our history with our families, our relationship with our parents, and our views on life and death. Regardless of the kind of relationship we have with our parents, their decline and eventual deaths rarely pass by as an insignificant event in our lives.

Wouldn't it be wonderful if we all could continue doing what we love for as long as we desire? Perhaps that is working in a career we are passionate about, gardening, running, golfing, playing tennis, knitting, reading and then, when we feel we are complete with our lives, we simply go to sleep and gently leave this world without any experience of pain or physical or cognitive decline. The reality is that most of us will not experience the aging process in this way. If we are fortunate enough to age long enough and be defined as "old," most likely we will encounter some bumps in the road that may be temporary or permanent. In varying degrees, we will need the assistance of others to keep us functioning as well as possible, for as long as possible. Perhaps it is your time now to be that assistance for one or both of your parents as they come face to face with physical and/or cognitive decline.

Chances are that you have been guided to this book because you are already involved with making decisions about when and how to help your parent(s). It would be ideal if we were prepared for such a journey prior to being immersed in it, but most of us don't want to even think about our parent's declining health, change in lifestyle, need for assistance, and the eventual grief we will experience when our parents die. I can still remember the first time my mom informed me that she was too tired to continue hosting the Thanksgiving holiday. I recall the sinking feeling of change that I felt, as I imagined in a flash, Thanksgiving happening in a different way. In my own mind it wouldn't be Thanksgiving at all if the meal didn't take place at my parent's home. But, our entire family was flexible and positive. We took turns hosting the event and sometimes took advantage of the delicious holiday brunches many restaurants offered. I adjusted to this "change," but at the same time it was a marker in time for me that I would have to adjust to the various "losses" that would arrive in increments.

The good news is that there are many professionals in the field of aging, like me, who have already done the homework for you and are eager to help and assist as you face the challenge of what can often be a very difficult and stressful time of life. Many people are shocked when they begin to deal with a parent who has become ill for any reason and feel as if they have entered a world of uncertainties and unknowns; such as, the geriatric ward of a hospital, a skilled nursing facility, home health-care nurse, assistive devices, Medicare issues, health directives. "All of this" is a stark contrast in comparison to a life of dropping children off at school, going to soccer games, dealing with work and business issues, socializing with friends, or relaxing by the fire with a glass of wine as you reflect on the day's activities.

Many people feel overwhelmed and in need of direction to determine which resources apply to their particular situation and how to face and deal with the often overwhelming emotions that accompany this stressful time. A major contributing factor in dealing with the difficult emotions that arise when our parents become ill is the lack of hope that things will get better. It is often a roller-coaster ride of ups and downs; not knowing whether to hope for wellness or let go and grieve for what is inevitable loss.

The intention of this book is to offer resources, direction, and an explanation for what may be happening with you and your family. In addition, when people begin to care for their aging parents, it can often serve as a time of profound self-discovery and personal growth. When I speak to audiences of caregivers, and they share the challenges they are facing with their families, I am always reminded that the journey of caregiving occurs within the context of the family's story. The dynamics in the family will become magnified and obvious. It's as if the family members walk backstage and put on the costumes they once wore to play the role they did when they were younger. This leaves many feeling confused, angry, depressed, and frustrated. Perhaps you are feeling like your family is a crazy and dysfunctional mess. That may indeed be true, but more than likely, all of you are reacting from a place of fear. Fear of change, fear of loss, fear that you can't be there the way you think you should. You may have tremendous concern that you won't have the help and support a person often needs to get through this challenging time.

In addition, this book offers information about how to integrate complementary and alternative medicine and holistic modalities into your and your parent's plan for care--essential tools to help you face the many challenges that lie ahead and improve quality of life for all. My hope is that this book will bring you a sense of calmness amongst the chaos in a way where you feel comforted by knowing others have taken the journey and empathize with you. While the details and characters in each of our lives are unique, our human reactions and emotions are generally universal; this is the beauty in how we are able to help one another during challenging times. Fortunately, many of us have traveled the path you are now facing, both with our own parents and in the professions we have chosen. Like a tour guide leading you through an unfamiliar forest, it is our passion to ease the way for you as you embark upon your own journey. A part of my personal story and experience, as well as the experiences of others, is shared in hopes of helping you know that you are not alone with the challenges you may be facing. These stories are shared to inspire you; to offer you hope and strength during your caregiving journey.

Unresolved grief ran deep in my family, and in both my mom and dad's families of origin. My grandmother was born in 1898 and was traumatized by many of her life experiences: war, the death of her young siblings, her brothers dominating her and bringing her to the United States from Italy (where her heart remained), and her husband's death in his early fifties. My dad was a jazzman who began playing the saxophone in bars when he was just twelve-years-old in the late 1930s. The older band mates would sneak him in and such began his introduction to cigarettes and alcohol. Later, he was accepted to The Juilliard School of Music, but his family convinced him that his life as a musician would lead to nowhere and he should pursue a degree in law. He allowed his dream to become a dormant and distant memory, but his repressed creative abilities haunted him for the remainder of his life to greater and lesser degrees. My dad lost his father when he was newly married in his early twenties. My mom lost her mother when she was twenty-two, shortly after my dad's father died. My mom also suffered five miscarriages prior to my older brother being born. My parents were ill equipped to cope with all of this grief, even though they had a beautiful home and a supportive social life in Pennsylvania.

Seeking better financial opportunities, my parents and brother relocated to California in 1961. My mom went along with the plan, but never adjusted or felt at home in California. My childhood was filled with my mom's tears of homesickness and her grief of losing babies, her mother, and her sister disowning her. My dad began drinking too much as life in Los Angeles took a toll on our family. When my mom's father died in 1965, experiencing and absorbing my mom's unresolved grief became a way of life for me. When my dad stopped coming home from work for dinner, and instead arrived past midnight after a night of drinking, my mom's grief and anguish became my problem to solve. She began to drink to cope with his absence and her pain, and sadly imposed her fears of my dad being dead in the street somewhere on my brother and me. I was about four-years-old when these seeds were planted deep within my psyche, and I lived in terror that I would lose my daddy forever.

When my dad received his terminal diagnosis, I knew I was facing the greatest fear of my entire life. My life had travelled full circle. I had worked hard on myself, I was strong, and I was helping others with their grief. I asked, "Why me, why my dad?!" I had to answer, "Why not, you've known this was coming for thirty-four years?" What was to come was the most difficult three years of my life, but also the most beautiful, rewarding, and liberating experience I could have imagined.

"And now here is my secret, a very simple secret;
it is only with the heart that one can see rightly,
what is essential is invisible to the eye."

ANTOINE DE SAINT-EXUPERY

CHAPTER ONE

One Hot, July Day
My Life Changed Forever

*I*t was the summer of 2000, and we were in the middle of a major heat wave in Southern California. The Fourth of July weekend had just passed, and I was booked solid with appointments well into the evening. I had so many errands to run that day that I grabbed my lunch out of the office refrigerator and decided to eat it in the car. It was more than 100 degrees as I started my car and began listening to my cell phone messages while I blasted the air conditioner trying to cool off the car. One of the messages was from my mom. She was sobbing as she tried to inform me that the doctor had called to tell my dad he had a tumor in his lung. Both of my parents had been smokers for more than fifty years so we simply knew the final diagnosis would be what already sounded so violent to me, "lung cancer." As I tried to gather myself to call my parents, my world was spinning, my hands were shaking, and my car ran out of gas. I knew they needed my call of support, that was my role with them, but I already felt as if I was five-years-old being told my daddy was dying. I knew right then my life would never be the same.

Both of my parents had been functioning with emphysema, with the assistance of inhalers. I was watching for signs of decline and trying to gauge when I would need to offer my assistance, but nothing had prepared me for this. Just the day before, they had gone shopping, enjoyed lunch out, and laughed out loud as they shared the day with me during our nightly phone call. The car running out of gas almost seemed symbolic. My life had come to a screeching halt, and I had to gather my strength and begin to deal with what was for me the most emotionally intense time of my life. I gathered myself and called my parents; then I called to cancel my appointments for the rest of the day.

It was the kind of day that remains etched in your mind forever--the weather, what you ate, who hugged you when you cried, what you were wearing--and the enormity of a situation that you know is going to change your life forever. I had grown up the child of alcoholic parents. I was the typical pleasing, co-dependent, hyper-vigilant daughter that was on a mission to help my parents stop drinking for my entire childhood. They had been sober for eighteen years; not because I succeeded, but because my dad nearly died from abusing alcohol. Fear got the best of them, and they quit drinking and never looked back.

I had been "off-duty" in my mind since that time. My enormous and emotionally crippling childhood fear of "losing my daddy" had been put to rest for years. After AAA came to put gas in my car, I broke down and cried. I had an awful feeling I was now going to face the dreaded monster face to face. I was suddenly called to be on active duty; save my dad's life and save my mom from losing my dad, which saves me from having to take care of my mom emotionally. That was the theme of my life--the painful and difficult truth that ultimately set me free from the entanglements of my family of origin.

My parent's decline in health and eventual deaths became a journey of resolution and liberation for me. This did not happen in a day, a month, or even in a year. It has been a profound journey of continually discovering who I am "underneath it all."

Caring for your parents may offer you the time to re-examine your family relationships, the false beliefs you have about yourself and others, and the baggage you may be carrying within you. If you have the courage to embark on this journey with an open heart and mind, you just may emerge from the experience a freer, happier, and a more joyful and fulfilled person than you ever could have imagined before.

REALIZING YOUR PARENTS NEED HELP

Without a doubt, caring for parents in declining health is often a marathon and not a sprint. It can be difficult to know how to pace yourself for a journey whose length is unknown. Often we are already doing our best to balance the wheel of life--demanding careers, children, spouses, partners, and personal health--while trying to remain connected to important long-term friends, when suddenly life turns upside down with the realization that our once independent parent(s) needs our assistance; maybe not just once or twice, but for the remainder of their lives.

This scenario is becoming more and more common as we are able to live longer lives while managing chronic diseases that used to take our lives quickly. It is reported that the percentage of adult children who are caring for their parents has tripled since 1994. Many people, especially women, age fifty or more, leave the work force early to care for a parent who is in ill health (*Wall Street Journal*, June 2011). Caregivers also suffer high rates of depression, symptoms of stress, and are more likely to consume alcohol excessively. It's imperative that family caregivers arm themselves with information, assistance, and awareness about their own health needs.

Under the best of circumstances, we feel honored to help our parent(s) who is in declining health, but being a caregiver to our parents can stretch our limits physically and emotionally. It may be the first time it occurs to you that you will not have your parents around forever. It is wise to take care of your own feelings of loss and sadness; it doesn't mean you are giving up hope on your parent or of having future quality time. Most often we are not prepared for this time of life; we'd rather not think about it, or we hope it won't "happen" to us. Communicating about, and planning for, a parent's changing needs is not always a pleasant conversation, and is often avoided until a crisis occurs.

The good news is that due to a booming older adult population there is an increasing interest in the lives of those sixty-five-years of age and older. There are more senior living communities than ever before, more resources and information for assistance, and more awareness about caregiving, both professional and family caregiving. It may be that the realization that your parent's need for help has come on suddenly. It may also be that the need for assistance is the result of a slow decline: small strokes, not eating well, isolation, dementia, heart disease, COPD, Parkinson's disease.

Being prepared and aware can offer us the best chance to preserve quality time and maintain healthy relationships in our families.

WHOSE LIFE IS IT ANYWAY?

There are numerous health scenarios that may knock on the door of any of us and rob us of our ability to live life the way we are accustomed. It usually doesn't work out well when a person feels as if their child is moving in and taking over their lives. Most of us want to remain as independent as possible, for as long as possible, therefore, be aware that there are ways to communicate that work better than others when it comes to "helping" your parents as they age.

If you are noticing a decline in your parent's ability to function, it's important and helpful to evaluate the situation and respond in a sensitive manner to do what is most beneficial to your parent's quality of life. A tremendous challenge in navigating through this time of life can be balancing difficult and intense emotions, while simultaneously being practical and calm as you manage these situations.

WHERE DO I BEGIN? ASSESSING YOUR PARENT'S NEEDS AND DESIRES

The first step is assessing your parent's particular situation by becoming aware of their abilities, as well as their possible limitations. You may discover that they are functioning better or worse than you had assumed. It is best if you "assess" in a quiet, respectful way and simply make observations about your parent's routine and health status. Assisting and helping can happen later, unless it is an emergency situation. The following are some suggestions about what you will want to consider and/or observe.

ACTIVITIES OF DAILY LIVING (ADL'S)

This refers to how your loved one is able to care for themselves and maneuver through their day. For example, is your mother able to bathe herself without assistance or get herself dressed? Is she able to do her own grocery shopping and keep her home clean and in order? Is she paying her bills on time? Many older adults fear that if their abilities slip, they'll end up losing their autonomy or worse yet, end up in a "nursing home." As a result, they feel they better hide the truth about needing help. There are many ways to assist a person who is having trouble with ADL's, which this book covers. Some serious warning signs are a yard that has become overgrown, a neglected pet, unopened mail, ordering excessive items online, utilities or telephone being turned off due to lack of payment, or bruises and cuts (may be secretly falling). However, be aware that skin often becomes thinner with age and excessive bruising can result with even a small bump that a younger person wouldn't even notice. You will also want to observe how your parent is walking. Does it appear as if they are in pain or weak? Pain or weakness could put them at risk for a fall, which is a very serious and common risk factor for older adults.

WHERE WILL MY PARENTS LIVE?

It will be very important for you to hear your parent's desires about where they wish to live when it comes time for them to need some assistance. Most people insist they want to remain living in their own home for the duration of their lives or for at least as long as they can. This may mean hiring a professional caregiver, either part or full time to assist them, keep them safe, and offer *you* peace of mind. It is also quite likely that your mother or father, unless they have visited friends in a facility, are not aware of the changes in senior housing options. This is also a conversation that will be revisited over time.

When we are healthy, it's much easier to express the desire to remain where we are comfortable and familiar. However, if our health declines we may change our mind about where we feel safe. If your parent insists on staying home, expect resistance when you discuss the need to hire a caregiver. (Chapter 5 discusses meeting this "resistance for assistance.") It's important to discuss the option, if one exists, for a parent to move in with a family member. Also, how involved are your parents in the community, do they need to remain close to their current physician, and what would be most beneficial to them to preserve their quality of life? For example, if they have a beloved pet, it's not compassionate to move them to a facility that doesn't allow pets. At this stage of life, an older adult has most likely suffered their share of loss and having to endure the loss of a pet is simply not fair if it can be avoided.

IS MY PARENT'S HOME SAFE?

You'll want to honestly assess your parent's safety. Things to consider are getting up and down the stairs safely, does the bathroom have properly installed grab bars in the shower and around the toilet, is there a non-slip surface in the shower, can your parent get up a small set of porch stairs leading to the front door, is there excessive clutter, have they fallen recently or made errors when taking medication? Again, helping your parent avoid a fall is a priority. You can go online and download a safety checklist form to assist you with a safety assessment (please refer to the Resources section). There are also ways to remind a person electronically to take medication. Chapter Two covers the various forms of what is called "gerotechnology," an expanding field of options designed to assist people in living independently for as long as possible.

IS DRIVING SAFE?

Try your best to determine if your parent's driving ability has declined. Do they mention getting lost or losing the car? Have they had more than one fender bender? (Privately check the car for dents and scratches.)   Are they able to see over the dashboard?   Can they turn their head to look for oncoming traffic or pedestrians? Can they reach the controls on the dashboard? Are they able to get in and out of the vehicle safely? Do they remember to put the car in park and remove the keys? If not, it may be time to consider a modified car or other transportation options.   Driving is discussed in greater length in Chapter Two.

DECLINING HEALTH

Does your parent have unexplained weight loss? This could be due to not having enough energy to do the grocery shopping on a regular basis or perhaps they don't have enough energy to cook the food and clean up the dishes. Ask them when they last went to the dentist as they may be having tooth pain, an oral infection, or improperly fitting dentures. An oral infection can be a serious threat to a person's over-all health. There may also be underlying health conditions that need immediate attention such as dementia, cancer, depression, or emphysema, to name a few.

HEARING AND EYESIGHT

Is your parent having difficulty hearing and seeing? If you don't know, find out the last time your parent had an eye and hearing exam. Hearing loss is a major cause of depression and isolation. In addition, ensure your parent receives a thorough eye exam to check changing eyesight, as well as to check for presence of disease, such as glaucoma or cataracts.

DO YOU SUSPECT DEMENTIA?

The most common form of dementia is Alzheimer's disease. The name comes from the German physician, Alois Alzheimer, who first described the brain disease in 1906. As many as 5.4 million Americans have the disease, and it is the 7th leading cause of death in the United States. Risk factors for the disease are genetics, diabetes (insulin resistance), cardiovascular disease, traumatic brain injury, depression, declining estrogen levels, and current smoking (Alzheimer's Association, Orange County, CA).

Our brains do change as we age. We may notice that it takes us longer to remember things or our thinking may be slower. However, serious mood and behavioral changes, memory loss, confusion, or other major changes taking place in the way our mind works is not normal and should be addressed as soon as possible.

It can be difficult to determine if a person is experiencing benign forgetfulness or showing a decline in cognitive functioning. It is also important to note that certain conditions often mimic the signs of dementia. For example, drug interactions, incorrect dosage of a medication due to loss of weight, urinary tract infection, dehydration, depression, or a head injury from a fall. It is imperative that a proper diagnosis be made through a medical evaluation. There are medications and treatments that may slow the progression of the disease. The topic of a family member dealing with a loved one who is suffering from dementia is expansive. The following is an excerpt from Rosemary De Cuir's book, *Coping with Dementia: What Every Caregiver Needs to Know* (2007), as well as from the Alzheimer's Association (www.alz.org).

Some of the ways in which a decline in cognitive functioning is characterized are:

- Difficulty discussing thoughts, principles, and opinions
- Lack of attention to details, such as mail left out for days, unpaid bills, decline in self-care
- Hoarding, hiding valuables, erratic behavior
- Imagined conversations
- Neglected home, yard, or pets
- Withdrawal from activities that were previously enjoyed
- Inability to perform tasks to completion, such as cooking, driving, paying bills
- Difficulty reading or putting an outfit together

- Usual rituals are ignored, such as not taking medications, not observing holidays, skipping church after many years of attendance
- Misplacing things and losing the ability to retrace steps
- Decreased or poor judgment
- Memory disrupts daily life
- Confusion with time or place
- Changes in mood or personality
- Challenges in planning or solving problems
- New problems with words in speaking or writing

It is important to be aware of new relationships that your loved one may have. When an older adult is confused and/or lonely and isolated, they are especially vulnerable to manipulative people who know how to appear "helpful" while emptying bank accounts and taking advantage of seniors whose families are uninvolved or live at a distance. In addition, check credit card statements for charges that are suspect. If your parent has reached a point where they can no longer use credit cards properly, it's best to destroy the cards before irreparable damage is done. If an outsider has gained access to bank accounts, notify the bank and close the accounts (De Cuir, 2007).

DEPRESSION

Aging often involves losses; some of which include: spouse, friends and siblings, identity through retirement, physical mobility, cognitive decline, financial instability, home, and loss of privacy and independence. Any of these situations may cause depression. Becoming isolated for an older adult is very problematic, and can cause depression and "crabbiness." Perhaps your parent is grieving the loss of their spouse or partner even if they died many years ago. Many of their friends may have also passed away. Day after day of being alone, not being able to drive, having physical pain, not being able to do the things they love to do, not being able to shower as much as they'd like, not having the energy to cook for themselves, contributes to depression. Loss takes a tremendous toll on a person's psyche and will to live. Someone stopping by for an hour or two a couple of times a week to drop off groceries is simply not enough to remedy a person's sense of feeling isolated. Your mother or father may not even realize they feel this way and will tell you they are fine. They may interpret and accept what they are experiencing as being "old and tired." It may not be possible for you to spend any more time with your parent, but be open to other solutions.

Let's remember that our current generation of seventy or eighty year-olds is probably not accustomed to expressing their feelings openly. Generally speaking, they are a tough bunch that survived, what may seem to them, to be much worse than "growing old." I have noticed that we often become so hyper focused on an older adult's physical health and managing all the symptoms that often go with the various conditions, that we forget to pay attention to the fact that as we all age, our emotions and how we feel about things remains intact. I have yet to see a support group in an assisted living facility that addresses the possible crisis of adjustment an older adult may be experiencing after moving from their home of possibly forty years. Rather than talking about feelings that often resolve over time naturally when acknowledged and honored, our culture often medicates people so they may continue to conform to the routine that is convenient for the caregivers.

WHAT CAN YOU DO?

- Open a discussion about the possibility of attending activities at the local senior/community center.
- If your parent is no longer driving, check to see what public transportation for older adults is available in their community.
- Become aware of local Adult Day Care centers.
- Don't be afraid to ask them how they feel. You can simply ask: "Mom, are you happy?" "What can I do to help?" "Do you feel

lonely?" "Would you be open to trying something new?" "I am more than happy to look into that for you."

- Consider if your parent has a hearing impairment, and try to schedule an exam. Hearing loss can add to feelings of isolation and be the cause of many older adults withdrawing from social activities. Try to be patient and educate yourself on how to cope with a loved one who has hearing loss. There are numerous styles and ranges of cost for hearing aids.
- Ask your parent when they last had a physical exam and encourage one if it's overdue.
- Be sure your parent is having their eyes examined at least once a year.
- Be sure they are receiving dental care. A lack of oral health can lead to other serious issues in the body.

• FINANCES/LEGAL ISSUES

It will be important to know your parent's financial situation. This will determine their long-term plan. For example, many people don't realize until they are faced with a health crisis that Medicare does not pay for non-medical in-home care and assistance for activities of daily living. In addition, Medicare only covers the care a person may need in a nursing home for a limited amount of time and not for the duration of a person's life. You will also want to know what insurance policies they have, bank accounts, rental agreements, and any other business paperwork or contracts. Getting important legal documents in order is also important. Chapter Two covers this topic in greater detail.

• HEALTH STATUS

Have you met your parent's primary care physician and/or any specialist they may be seeing for a chronic health condition? If they do have a condition, it is important that you become aware of the prognosis so you can help your parent plan for future care.

You will want to ensure that you or whoever is designated as the primary caregiver has the power of attorney to make decisions in case they are unable to do so for themselves (see important documents).

NOW WHAT?

After you have a clear idea of what you and your parents are dealing with, you'll want to locate resources and proceed calmly and respectfully. At all times remember you are there to support and to help them maintain their quality of life and independence for as long as possible. Depending upon the nature of your parent's challenge, consider that they may improve and get better. Needing your assistance may be temporary, but a good opportunity to get things in place for later care.

My dear friend's mother, Marge was diagnosed with late stage uterine cancer. During surgery, the tumor was accidently dropped into her abdominal cavity as it was being removed, making the situation even more complicated. In addition, she developed a post-operative infection that nearly took her life. A few months later her husband died. Marge then decided to sell her home and relocate to another state to be close to her grandchildren. That was nearly ten years ago and Marge is now eight-two, healthy and living independently in her own home. My friend is prepared for the day when her mother will need her assistance again, but for now is grateful that she is healthy and doing well. Try not to give up hope on your parent; while their health may falter frequently, they may enjoy many more quality years after coping with and surviving a health crisis.

"We are so used to our parents taking care of us, taking care of our children, being our rock of support. Suddenly, it changes. One of them gets sick and the other one is incapable of coping with the situation, so we step in."

SALLY QUINN

CHAPTER TWO
Remember To Listen

I began to notice that my parents were "slowing down." They seemed more short of breath, my dad was reluctant to drive long distances, and they both began to take a long time in the morning to get ready for the day. I was "feeling" that changes were not far away, but wasn't quite sure how to open a discussion. I decided it would be best to allow it to happen naturally in an informal setting. About once a month I would drive out to see my parents, and we would go to breakfast or lunch and talk about a variety of topics ranging from politics, to spirituality, to health, to my working life, to my dad's working life, and back again. The way I eased myself into "the conversation" was to discuss an older client I had who had become quite ill. I used that as an opener to ask my dad how long he planned to continue working and if they were okay financially. Because they were still relatively healthy, I was able to frame it in a way of, "If something happens and you're not able." Rather than, "You are no longer able to care for yourself." Fortunately for me they were very touched that I cared enough to ask and the conversation was extremely positive and set us up for what was to follow. However, there were many other situations and discussions that were not as graceful; in fact, they were heartbreaking, and I felt ill equipped to manage them. I was in no way prepared and couldn't find a book like this one to ease the way. I realized that I was facing obstacles because I felt like I had to know all the answers right now and know what to do at all *times. As a result, I wasn't listening and allowing the situation and my parents to reveal to me how to best help.*

Upon my dad's diagnosis, and in my panic, I insisted that my parents move closer to me so I could help. My brother and his wife were busy raising their children and in truth, I believed that only I would know how to help them the "right way." They eventually did move, making it easier for me to be with them often and be of more help. If I had it to do over, I would listen better to their concerns, their needs, and their true desires. Maybe they still would have moved to be closer, but I would know they did so because they wanted to, not because I insisted they do so just for me. In retrospect, I realize my mom probably felt like she was moving from Pennsylvania to California again; all for someone else.

After my dad passed away, my mom expressed on a daily basis that she did not want to continue living in the same apartment. I kept insisting that in time she would change her mind and that the apartment was a good place for her to live. It took me several weeks to finally listen to her and talk about it. I realized that in truth, the grief and exhaustion I was feeling over losing my dad left me drained, cranky, and in no mood to pack everything up and move my mom again. However, ultimately my mom's decision to move empowered her, and I'm convinced it offered her more quality days for the time she had left. A couple of times a week I would pick her up and we would go apartment hunting and then have lunch together. My mom married my dad at age twenty-two and had never lived with anyone else except for her parents, my dad, and eventually me and my brother.

At age seventy-three she was making a statement about her independence. I gained a respect for my mom that I previously didn't have. Because she had been so dependent, I had expected her to give up and die after my dad's death, but here she was making decisions on how to make the best of my dad being gone and knowing, without a doubt, what she needed to do next. We found her a wonderful apartment in a neighborhood she loved. It was a special time for us, as we mindfully hung pictures, chose new bedding, and a new, more "feminine" sofa. She was as content as she could be under the circumstances, but more importantly, she felt empowered and in control of her own life.

PLANNING FOR CARE

WHERE DO I BEGIN?

What do you do if you are already in the middle of a crisis and you and your parents have not put a plan in place detailing the actions to be taken if their health declined? The answer is that it is never too late to develop a plan. If you are reading this book then you are already in the process of gathering information and deciding where to go from here. The reality is that very few people plan for dealing with their parent's aging process. How a person's "old age" will look is seldom apparent until they arrive in the place of needing assistance. Planning, caring for, and being proactive is most often crisis driven and needs based.

IMPORTANT DOCUMENTS:

Put a three ring binder together containing your parent's important documents (or copies), including their legal and health information. This way everything is readily available in one place so important paperwork doesn't become misplaced, and you can easily find what you need when you need it. Having to scramble and look for things will only add to your level of stress. For example, many people will keep their healthcare directives and other important information in their safe deposit boxes. It's fine to keep copies there, but if the document is needed in a crisis and no one has access to it, this is a problem. The person, as well as the alternates, ought to have copies of directives so they can protect, advocate for, and act on wishes. Your parent(s) may already have taken care of important documents and have an attorney who will handle their affairs. If this is the case, ask your parent to supply you with the attorney's contact information, and anything else you may need to know, so you may properly assist them in a time of need.

ESTATE PLANNING

A person's "will" is the main document for transferring property when a person dies. If we die without a will in place, the state law where we reside will control how the property is distributed. Find out if your parents have an estate plan in place. Experts agree that a well-drawn plan addresses the following areas:

The Will - Even if your parent(s) don't have extensive belongings, it's important to allocate what they do have according to their wishes. This will hopefully avoid family conflict and arguing over items as well. If your parents have a large estate, a will may also help reduce taxes. If both of your parents are living, they should each have their own will to avoid complications. If the estate is extensive, you may want to use a lawyer to ensure it is drafted properly. You can also purchase generic wills (and other forms) at stationery stores or download them from the web; however, many professionals caution that the verbiage on these generic forms may not be precise enough in some instances. All of the legalities involved are beyond the scope of this book; please seek the advice of a trusted lawyer when you are in doubt as to what is in the best interest of your parent. You may want to hire an elder law attorney; an attorney who practices or specializes in the legal issues primarily pertaining to older adults. If your parent's will was done many years ago (more than ten), you may suggest they have it reviewed by an elder law attorney in order to make any necessary changes.

Executor - The will should name an executor of the estate who's responsibilities are filing the will in probate court, distributing assets, filing and paying taxes, paying debts and expenses, and distributing life insurance and retirement plan funds.

Trusts - A trust is a legal document that can be used to mange property during a person's lifetime in the event of incapacity. It directs the management and distribution of property after death, creates long-term plans (education funds, for example), and often provides money to help another person or disabled child. **Living Trusts** can reduce administration fees and probate delays as well as reduce estate taxes. (Hall, 2011).

Durable Power of Attorney for Finances (DPA) - This document will authorize another person to act on your parent's behalf if they become incapacitated. If your parent(s) has this document in place ensure that the person authorized to make these decisions is still the appropriate one. Circumstances change through the years and it may be time to revisit this and create a new one. This authorizes the appointed person to sign checks to pay bills or make decisions regarding housing choices. Having this document in place will help your family avoid going to court to obtain guardianship over your parent's finances and care. Experts agree that it is best to have an attorney assist in getting this document in place. In addition, they caution that a DPA is not useful in every situation. It is important to know that it becomes ineffective upon a person's death.

Advanced Health Care Directive - This document expresses in writing what a person's healthcare wishes are. For example, what a person desires in regard to life-sustaining treatment. It also appoints a trusted person to make health care decisions when the person is unable to make decisions for themselves. *We should all have one of these in place **before** we are ill or in an accident.* The document can be completed without a lawyer. Hospitals and doctor's offices usually have them or you can download the document from the web. In addition, most office supply stores carry them. As with other important documents, if your parent(s) put an advanced healthcare directive in place many years ago, they may want to review it. Often, a person's feelings change about what is important to them in this regard as the years pass by.

Do not Resuscitate (DNR) - In medicine, a "**do not resuscitate**" or "**DNR**", sometimes called a "**No Code**", is a legal order written either in the hospital or on a legal form to respect the wishes of a patient not to undergo CPR or advanced cardiac life support (ACLS) if their heart were to stop or they were to stop breathing. A DNR does not affect treatment, other than that which would require intubation or CPR. When a person is very old, has multiple medical problems or advanced stage cancer, for example, they may wish to have a DNR in place to allow them to have a natural death and not be revived.

POLST - *Physician Orders for Life-Sustaining Treatment* - There are different POLST forms for each state. The form is a physician's order that outlines a plan of care, which reflects the patient's wishes concerning end-of-life care. For example, in California, it is a bright pink form that contains orders regarding life-sustaining wishes when a person becomes seriously ill. As the name of the document suggests, a physician must fill-out this form for it to be valid. The POLST form asks:

- Preferences for resuscitation
- Medical conditions
- Use of antibiotics
- Artificially administered fluids and nutrition

IMPORTANT NAMES, ACCOUNT NUMBERS, PHONE NUMBERS, AND ADDRESSES TO COLLECT:

- All doctors, dentists, and other health care professionals
- Medical information, including medications and dosages, health conditions
- Attorneys, accountants, insurance agents, real estate agents, financial advisors
- Banking information
- Close friends and relatives of your parents
- Religious or other spiritual information
- Clubs or organizations
- Certificate of Births, Marriage, Divorce, and Citizenship
- Veterans paperwork
- Insurance policy information (health, disability, long-term care, homeowner's, automobile, etc.)
- Copies of Social Security, Medicare, Medicaid (if applicable) cards

OTHER IMPORTANT INFORMATION TO GATHER:

- Real estate deeds
- Rental agreements
- Know where valuables are kept
- List of credit cards, debit cards
- Passwords to accounts/PIN numbers
- Tax returns
- How to care for the home and pets

- Have funeral arrangements been pre-paid; what are the burial or cremation desires?
- A list of all bills
- A list of assets
- A list of debts

All of us are more willing to trust when we feel as if we have been understood. As humans, we want to feel cared about and that our happiness matters.

DIFFICULT CONVERSATIONS, PEOPLE, AND SITUATIONS

What family caregivers seem to need help with most often is communication. They are simply at a loss, feeling discomfort and fear, with how to have a conversation with their parents that may be taken the wrong way, or may seem as if they are trying to take control of their parent's lives. It can be difficult to face what is really going on, and we hope the situation will just go away by itself. As difficult as it may be to have conversations about finances, health, living options, and advanced directives, waiting until a crisis occurs will only make it more difficult, if not impossible. The following are some examples of how to begin these difficult conversations. You can adjust the wording so that you are comfortable with what is appropriate for your situation. It may feel less threatening if you open the conversation in the form of a question. This sends the message that you care about what your parent may be thinking or feeling. After asking a probing question and before you respond, remember to listen to what your parent is expressing. Try to be present and sincerely interested in learning more about their concerns and desires. So often we ask a question and have already decided how we will respond before we hear the other person out. **Conversations:**

- *"Mom, have you thought about what you would want if your health became such that you are no longer able to live at home alone?"* This may lead into a conversation about having a professional caregiver at home or eventually moving into an assisted living facility. Chapter Eight explains the different living options.
- *"Dad, I am in the process of updating my will and my advanced directive for healthcare. It made me wonder if you have done this yet or do you want to update yours?"*
- *"Don't you think it's important for everyone to put their wishes in writing so what they want and don't want can be respected and honored?"*
- *"Mom, given your diagnosis, don't you think we should talk about how I (we) can be of support to you and plan ahead?"*
- *"Dad, how do you feel about your driving?"* *"I know how important your independence is to you, but do you think it is still safe for you to drive?"* Some adult children accompany their parent to a doctor's appointment and have the discussion with the doctor in a practical unemotional manner.
- *"Mom, we truly want to support your desire to remain in your own home, but if you don't allow us to help you choose a professional caregiver to help you, it's not going to be possible."* *"Why don't we just try it out for a few hours a week?"* *"We won't allow anyone to be here that you are not comfortable with, and who knows, you may make a new friend."*
- *"Mom and Dad, don't you think it will give us all peace of mind if we know what all of the housing options and costs are so we can plan in a calm manner?"* *"I'm happy to help you gather the information."*

Choose a time to talk with your parent when you know they are not tired, and you are not rushed. Most likely, you will be opening the door for a conversation that will be ongoing and possibly evolve over time. If your parent did an Advanced Directive for Healthcare twenty-years-ago, you may want to ask them if their thinking has changed on certain things. If you are comfortable, you may want to share with them how you feel about having life support or a feeding tube. When faced with difficult discussions my mom would commonly say, "Let's talk about nice things." I would sometimes tease her and ask her if she'd been on "It's a Small World" lately; her favorite ride at Disneyland. This helped to keep a serious and painful topic tolerable.

My parents did not make their burial wishes known until a few weeks before my dad's death. This only happened because my dad's hospice nurse insisted. This was a much darker experience for everyone involved than it would have been had this been handled when my dad was relatively well. I can still recall how guilty and grief stricken I felt that Saturday afternoon when I went to visit my parents after making funeral arrangements for my dad. It was even more heart wrenching as he held my face in his hands that day, looked deeply into my eyes, and told me how much he loved me. He knew his life was rapidly slipping away and our time together was limited. Again, had these details been dealt with sooner that moment of tender expression would have been relished without the feelings of guilt that I experienced.

My holistic health practice offered me many experiences of observing clients and their families go through the journey of facing life-threatening illnesses and end of life decisions. As a result, a couple of years prior to my own father's diagnosis of lung cancer, I did the best I could at the time to broach the difficult subject of end-of-life wishes with my parents. However, this was an area they were not open to discussing. In my opinion, it was due to their own unresolved grief of losing their own parents in very early adulthood. I had to back off and let it go, knowing that my brother and I would be dealing with it "when the time came." Sometimes we can only plant the seeds and hope a parent will come around and be open later to discussing it. Other times, it does become an urgent issue that must be handled. In my situation I had to say, "I know this is so very painful, I wish we weren't dealing with it, but 'Barbara,' the hospice nurse has called me a couple of times to ask what your wishes are for burial." I could barely get the word "burial" out of my mouth without breaking down. I tried to soften it by saying that it was just part of the hospice requirement to have burial or cremation plans in place.

I recently had the pleasure of overhearing a mother and her daughter's conversation at a restaurant. It took place in the late morning and both looked and sounded fresh. I couldn't help but overhear the daughter loudly, but respectfully, projecting her voice so her mother (obviously having difficulty with hearing) could understand what she was saying. This patient and loving daughter methodically explained to her mother, while writing everything down so they both could view the facts together, how much income she had, and what her monthly costs were to support her current situation. She then suggested several options for her mother to consider. I never heard the daughter tell her mother what she should or must do. It was a dignified and supportive conversation, based in reality that sent a loving message to the mother of care and protection.

Even though these conversations can often be difficult to begin, having them frees everyone to be a proactive participant rather than a victim of circumstance when something difficult happens. Like a surgeon who can't operate without surgical instruments, we need to be armed with knowledge and coping skills if we are to adequately handle and manage the stress often involved when one or both parent's health is declining.

PEOPLE AND SITUATIONS - *RON, HIS DAUGHTER AND THE CAR KEYS*

One of the most difficult challenges families often face is when a parent doesn't realize their driving is no longer safe. First, stop and think about how you would feel if you had to relinquish your car keys. Our ability to drive and go where we want, when we want is a priority for most of us. Driving represents freedom and autonomy. No matter our age, we all seem to remember the day we received our driver's license and the newly found feeling of freedom we felt. Ron was a retired lieutenant with the Los Angeles Police Department. I've known Ron and his family well for thirty years; his eldest daughter is one of my best friends. Ron was a man who took good care of his family; he was a leader, attentive and competent when it came to handling life. Unfortunately, this strong man who loved to golf, vacation, and spend time with his family was diagnosed with Parkinson's disease. Ron's daughter, Robin, observed the signs of decline in her father's driving ability as the disease progressed. She would remark to him, "Dad, at some point you won't be able to drive anymore." He would then acknowledge that he was aware that someday, off in the future, he would need to give up driving. Robin planted the seed and opened up this conversation early, before her dad had an incident. It is much less threatening and less upsetting when something is presented as a future event and not something to be dealt with immediately. Slowly, but surely Robin and her sisters began to notice that their father no longer turned his head to see what or who was behind him as he was backing up. His reaction times were slower; his confidence as a defensive driver had waned. When the subject would come up about not driving, Ron would say, "Yes, I know, but we're not there yet." Denial is common, and it can drag on for a long time. Robin and her sisters initially coped with this by gradually removing his opportunities to drive. They offered to pick him up and take him to the doctor, to lunch, shopping, etc. He wasn't completely aware that in large part, they were offering because they were concerned about his safety and the safety of others.

Eventually, Ron's ability to drive was severely impacted by his disease, and Robin decided it was necessary to express to him that it was no longer safe for him to drive. These are the moments when you feel that "role reversal" has occurred between you and your parent. Imparting sensibility, wisdom, and making a decision in the interest of safety for the one who protected and guided you, for so many years, can be a heartbreaking experience. Heartbreaking it was for Robin when her dad's eyes welled up with tears and he said, "Just give me a chance Rob, I can show you that I can do it." Robin explained that she would be devastated if he was hurt in an accident or he hurt someone else. She expressed to him, in a respectful manner, that she couldn't take that chance. She validated his feelings by saying, "I know this is so hard for you."

If this were a child you might ease the immediate desire by encouraging them to wait until next year, or wait until you grow an inch, or express that you have your entire life ahead of you. It is true, one of the most difficult realities of caring for our parents when their health is declining is that so often we know they will not get better, but get worse. We not only hurt for their losses, but for our own, as well. Fortunately, for this family, Ron was sad, but agreeable. He didn't snatch the keys and ride all over town sideswiping other vehicles or drive through store windows, as is so often the case. He adjusted and what made it bearable was his daughter's acknowledgment and validation that she knew it was so difficult for him to surrender this part of his independence. She shared that one day this will happen to her. What an equalizer and wonderful way to ease the pain of what is often a power struggle of, "I know what is best for you and you better listen."

WHAT IF MY PARENT WON'T STOP DRIVING?

Check to see if the city in which your parent lives offers driving evaluations and safe driver classes for seniors. If your mother or father simply refuse to do this, have a talk with their physician about your concerns. Request that the physician report it to the department of motor vehicles. In most states, they will require the person to take a driving test. It is quite common for people to know deep within themselves that they are not safe on the road; as a result, they may not take the test and stop driving on their own. They feel like it is their decision to stop, not someone else telling them they are incapable of driving. Under certain circumstances you may be morally forced to take the car keys away from your parent. They may be furious with you and even stop speaking to you for a time, but wouldn't you feel worse if they killed a child? You have to be strong and know what you are doing is the right thing even if they are mad at you. At the same time, have a plan in place for how they will get to doctors appointments, grocery shopping, and other errands. Take care to ensure that they have a way to continue to make their social events so they don't become isolated.

If you and other family members can't take turns getting them out of the house, it will be necessary for you to find other means of safe and reasonable transportation for them.

So often we are trying hard to find solutions that please everyone. Satisfying every person immediately is not always possible, but people do adjust, just like Ron. Do your best to accept that caring for your aging parent can be a difficult experience for all involved. Many adult children become frustrated because their parents don't cooperate. Remember, they may feel as if they are relinquishing life as they know it and death will soon follow. That scenario can feel very threatening.

GERIATRIC CARE MANAGER

If you live a significant distance away from your parent(s) or you and your siblings are having difficulty agreeing on a plan of action for care, you may want to hire a geriatric care manager to help you make decisions, mediate with family members, and coordinate valuable services and resources. A *certified* geriatric care manager is typically a registered nurse, a social worker, or case manager with a minimum of three years of experience in the field. Visit the website for the National Association of Professional Geriatric Care Managers (NAPGCM) to find a qualified GCM in your area (www.caremanager.org).

SUMMARY

Remember, whether you are in the beginning stages of preparing to assist your parent(s) or in the middle of a crisis, it is never too late to craft a plan that will help you get organized and free your mind of the chaos that develops due to feeling overwhelmed with a "to-do list" when you aren't quite sure what to do in the first place.

- Begin having conversations about planning.
- Get important documents in order (wills, advanced directives, power of attorney).
- Create a three-ring binder with documents; important health information; account numbers; important names, phone numbers, and

addresses; as well plan of care instructions which include: medication dosage, frequency and purpose, all health conditions, and daily schedule. It is helpful to include activity and food/beverage preferences and requirements, as well.

- Educate yourself about your parent's health condition(s) and prognosis, as well as helpful resources.
- Assess the situation. How well is your parent caring for him/herself? How well are they maintaining their home life? Evaluate the condition of: the refrigerator (rotting and expired food), the yard, their pets, cleanliness of home and themselves, clutter, disrepair.
- Are the bills going unpaid and is excessive mail unopened?
- Is their car scratched and/or dented?
- Do they get lost easily on familiar routes?
- Is there a marked decline in the way they normally function?
- Are they losing control of their finances? Traits to observe include: ordering excessive amounts of items online, being scammed by dishonest "salespeople," do they have any "new friends" overly interested in "helping" them.
- If they need help with their "activities of daily living" consider hiring a professional caregiving agency for a few hours a week to start.
- If possible, divide caregiving tasks with family members so no one person has to do it all.
- If you and other family members live far away from your parent(s) consider hiring a geriatric care manager to arrange and oversee their care.
- Remain aware and consider when "aging in place" is no longer a safe and wise option.
- See resources listed at the end of this book for a list of organizations, publications and other helpful sources.

"The mother-daughter relationship is the most complex."

WYNONNA JUDD

CHAPTER THREE
The Love And The Pain

*A*s *I previously mentioned, when my dad was first diagnosed with lung cancer, I knew without a doubt that I wanted my parents to move closer to me. It was clear that the 110 mile round trip drive would take its toll on me, as I made my way back and forth to assist them. However, there was more to consider than my own physical and emotional demands. My parents were living in an independent senior apartment. They absolutely adored their neighbors, the social events, and the community they had lived in for so many years. My brother, his wife, and their children were only a couple of miles away. "How much would they be able to help," I wondered? It was a very difficult decision to make, but eventually we all came to the conclusion that it was best for them to live closer to me because I had a more flexible schedule, no children, and more resources. This was the surface reason anyway; in my own mind I knew I would pour my heart and soul into caring for my parents the way I thought they **ought** to be cared for. I was the nurturer and the one that thought she knew best how to help. We'll never know for sure if that is true or not, but that is what I believed at the time. It may sound commendable or arrogant; either way, believing only you know best and not requesting some sort of help from others will take you down the path of assured caregiver burnout.*

I was the one who went grocery shopping, cleaned my mom's apartment, took her to the doctor, did the laundry, took time each day to leave work and have lunch with her, stop by her apartment after work and called several times a day in between all of that. My brother was the "Sandwich Man." After my dad died, my brother would visit my mom once a week and bring her a fancy, gigantic sandwich. She looked so forward to his visit. They never had any confrontation regarding the bills, the laundry, the grocery shopping, etc. Sometimes I felt resentful and hurt because of this. When the care recipient becomes frustrated or angry, they usually will take it out on the primary caregiver; it just seems to be how it works.

There exists plenty of scholarly literature explaining the complicated relationships between mothers and their daughters. Mothers tend to openly express displeasure and disappointment to their daughters, and daughters are constantly trying to win the approval of their mothers (Secunda, 1990). Competition, advice perceived as criticism, mothers trying to help their daughters not make the same mistakes they did; these are just some of the reasons given for the often strained relationship daughters have with their mothers. In my case, my mom and I had kept things quiet for several years; however, after my dad died, the buffer between us was removed and the painful strain between us resurfaced.

MY DAUGHTER, MY CAREGIVER

"The cultural ideal is that women are caring and selfless; thus, it is often assumed that adult daughters will make accommodations or sacrifices in their own lives to care for aging parents."

Daughters tend to be the ones who provide the day in, day out care. The meals, the bathing, the medications, the dressing, and the household maintenance while sons tend to be the ones who show up to watch sports, a movie, take the parent out to dinner, or simply sit and chat. Mothers, especially, may view their sons as heroes, experts, and allies and see their daughters as the nags and nuisances insisting on keeping them clean, well fed, and properly cared for in every way. It often equates to the experience of a weekend dad showing up to take the kids to the baseball game while mom ensures the homework gets done, and the children eat a healthy dinner. One geriatric case manager, Marsha Foley, created a support group in the Chicago area called "Dutiful Daughters, Sainted Sons." While she points out that some women have nothing to do with helping their parents and some sons are on the front lines assisting, more often than not, it is the daughter who provides the care. Studies reveal that adult daughters, navigating the territory of caregiving for their aging parents, may experience distressful feelings of guilt. Filial responsibilities are, however, often implicit and may vary across and within families based on factors such as race, ethnicity, socioeconomic status, and generation (Gonyea, Paris, de Saxe Zerden, 2008). Excessive feelings of guilt have the potential for leading to depression, as well as other psychological disorders. Foley points out that woman also have a tendency to experience guilt more often than men. It seems men are better at compartmentalizing, hiring others to take care of what needs to be done, and are simply more pragmatic in dealing with parents whose health is declining.

In my own situation, I had a very difficult time detaching from my feelings of anguish as I visualized my mom all alone in her apartment for the first time in her life. I would run the story over and over in my mind of my mom being so dependent on my dad, how much she must miss him, how isolated she must feel. I ran myself ragged trying to fill the gap and rescue my mom from feeling her grief. In retrospect, I realize that my efforts, as well intentioned as they were, were simply not reasonable. My work suffered, my friendships suffered, as did my relationship with my significant other. It is impossible to do it all without experiencing the consequences of having other areas of your life impacted.

Many women believe that it is their duty and role to nurture everyone else before they look after their own well-being. It is my belief that I went overboard because I thought I should be able to do it all because I didn't have children of my own and my brother did. In addition to this, when a family reconvenes to assist parents, it is common for previous roles to come into play once again. When my brother and I were children, our parents were abusing alcohol to the extent that there were many traumatic days and nights of danger for all of us. I was the child always attempting to intervene, help, make all the fighting stop; I truly believed I had that power at five-years-old. My brother, on the other hand, normally stayed in his room or, as he got older, left on his bicycle to avoid the chaos. These roles were robustly intact for our family as my parent's health began to decline.

Virginia Morris, author of *How To Care For Aging Parents,* warns siblings who are in the trenches helping their parent to beware of the "brother" who lives at a distance and flies in occasionally to check in on mom or dad. She describes them as usually having a little bit of knowledge about medicine or law, and as eager to let other siblings know about everything they are doing wrong and how to fix it. She advises to go along with what the "expert" is suggesting and offer him a ride to the airport when it's time for him to go home. Of course, this could easily be a "know it all" sister, as I witnessed several times in my homecare agency.

If you are a daughter, or daughter-in-law, in a family that expects you to do it all because you are the nurturer, the one who lives closest, the one without children, the one without the highest paying job, stop and take an internal survey of your physical, emotional, mental, and time limitations. No one can do this alone without serious consequences to their health and well-being. Many daughters-in-law approach me privately after I give a presentation on caregiving. They express that they are at a loss because they are expected to assist their husband's parents, but do not feel they have the same rights to express their concerns, or to speak up for themselves when they feel taken advantage of. They are very often resentful, and because they obviously do not have the same familial history with their husband's mother or father, they offer to help out of a sense of obligation to their spouse, not necessarily because they feel close and loving to their in-laws.

No matter what your role is in your family, realize that caregiving is a complex journey and reach out for support. Educate yourself about why you and other family members are reacting the way they are reacting. At the risk of generalizing, sons tend to be more task orientated and less emotional about what is going on with their parent. For example, if the money is handled and mom is safe in a facility, then sons think everything is okay. Daughters are more prone to worrying that their mother may be depressed, that the staff in the facility isn't treating her right, or "knows" her mother misses her home; as a result, daughters have a tendency to feel responsible for remedying what their mother may be feeling.

If you are a daughter or daughter-in-law, take heart and know you can adjust your perception and create a better experience for yourself. Please check the resources and recommended reading at the end of this book for more assistance.

"Every successful caregiving task has to start with clear communication."

KUBA

CHAPTER FOUR
Roles Emerge

*U*pon *learning of my dad's lung cancer, my mom emotionally crumbled, which destabilized her emphysema, making it necessary for her to be hospitalized. My parents had met in the fifth grade and my mom took such joy telling the story of how, on class picture day, she waited and watched to see where my dad would sit and then rushed to sit next to him. I still look at that picture in the family photo album. My mom and dad were more dependent on each other than was healthy. Leaning into the other for most every need, they had no social network of friends and resisted engaging the many wonderful people who were interested in befriending them during the later years of their lives.*

With my mom hospitalized, and my dad dealing with a likely terminal diagnosis, our entire family was reeling with grief, anger, sadness, denial, and desperation. My brother, intent on maintaining his own family normalcy, was away on vacation with his wife and two teenage children. I was the "unmarried" and the childless child who had the time and capacity to deal with our parents. During one particularly difficult day, my dad was undergoing a needle biopsy of his lung tumor in the same hospital where my mom was. I traveled back and forth from one area of the hospital to another checking on each. Unfortunately, during the needle biopsy, my dad's lung collapsed, and it became a major emergency. I literally ran the halls of the hospital trying to cover up the truth to my mom while comforting my dad and dealing with my own unraveling feelings of fear that I would soon lose my "daddy." I had become profoundly aware of just how fragile our lives really are. I had a recurring image running through my mind of a glass of water spilling and washing away and drowning an army of ants, as a result. That was how life's ability to change suddenly felt to me. Whether by natural disaster, an accident, a terminal diagnosis, or death; one moment we experience our world a certain way, and the next moment life may sweep us away without our awareness of the approaching shift in our reality.

I telephoned my brother to fill him in on what was happening at the hospital. I was annoyed that he wasn't as upset as I thought he "should" be. I interpreted this, and him being away on vacation, as him not caring about our parents or me. He expressed his concern for me by inviting me to join him and his family on the vacation saying, "It's close, if anything happens you can get back quickly." I nearly lost all sense of composer and stated back, "Something has happened, it is happening right now."

Through my own growth, healing, and formal education, I have realized, learned, and accepted that people cope with difficult circumstances in different ways. My role in my family of origin had always been to intervene, to help, to become involved, and to know what to do in times of crisis. While I was what you might call a first responder, my brother had always been a slow responder. I wasn't right and he wasn't wrong, we simply had differing styles in how we coped with the situation. Growing up, our home was very often filled with chaos and a lack of safety. As the resident "co-dependent," I believed I had the power to control the peace, make it better, and make it stop. When it didn't work, I also felt that it was my failure and would dig deeper to find a way to change the situation. I had begun my own life, my brother was married, and my mom and dad became wonderful grandparents to my niece and nephew. We had found a way to get along as a family and were all so grateful for my mom and dad's sobriety, new life, and good health. "Now, if they could just stop smoking," we would often remark. Upon my dad receiving the news that he had terminal lung cancer, I immediately sprang into action and put my uniform of co-dependence on. Once again, I had been called in for active duty.

Family issues, specific roles, anger, and hurt often lie dormant within a family for many years. Many families call a truce, so to speak, and create distance with family members. The distance may be geographic, emotional or both. When a parent's health declines, and it becomes necessary to see more of our siblings and parents, dormant and unresolved pain often reveals itself.

Since you are the family member who picked up this book, most likely you are an only child or like me, a first responder, a co-dependent, a pleaser, or the primary caregiver. An excellent way to preserve much needed energy is to realize early that there is no right way of responding to the situation of parents needing help. The way a person responds is their way, and quite simply, it is what it is, as they say. Beyond honest communication and requests for assistance, trying to make it any different will only exhaust you and rob you of hopefully having a rich and meaningful experience with your parents as you both age.

It took my own brother longer to assess and process what was happening with our parents. Once he and his wife did, we worked out ways in which we could all contribute to helping. We each had a unique journey that continues to play itself out today even though both of our parents have died.

I stayed with my dad the night he came home after recovering from his lung collapse. We had long talks about life and death and the emotions of fear that can often accompany a life-threatening experience. We spoke deeply of God, spirituality, and the definition of healing. With tears welling up in his eyes, my dad said to me, "When I do die, you will never need to worry about anything because I will always be watching out for you." While I know he's not able to interfere and help me win the lottery, I feel his love and guidance often. I was richly rewarded with numerous heart-swelling moments, such as the one I just shared. I would not trade that for anything.

"When a parent grows frail, roles shift uncomfortably, and both parent and child can become disorientated and unsure about how to behave."
Virginia Morris

FAMILY DYNAMICS

SIBLING RELATIONSHIPS

Many major decisions will need to be made during this stressful time of life. Often, siblings find themselves at odds with each other. They are already burdened by the pressures of their jobs, raising children, and doing their best to take care of the relationship they have with their spouse or significant other. It is usually a lack of mature communication that creates a breakdown in the family, possibly causing irreparable damage. The "burden" of care often falls on one sibling. This may be due to geographic location, specific circumstances, or established roles set by the family years prior. Regardless of the reasons why one sibling does more than another, one almost always emerges as the primary caregiver. It is important for children to divide the responsibilities according to ability, desire, and availability for completing the task while bearing in mind what is in the best interest of the mother or father (Morse & Quinn-Robbins, 1998). If your brother or sister is more of a paperwork person, it's probably best for them to deal with insurance issues, real estate, and bank accounts. Bear in mind that the sibling fulfilling this role may not be having the same emotional experience as you. It is natural for us to want others to suffer with us and share the pain of the experience. Pragmatic people often compartmentalize and may not "seem" to care as much as a feeling based person does. Do your best to let go of what and how you think your sibling should be behaving; it will save you from much frustration and grief.

As previously mentioned, many families have unresolved issues, resentment, anger, and emotional pain that has remained dormant for years. It can rise up like an ugly monster when the time comes to deal with parents who need help. It is important to acknowledge that it is a difficult time for all involved and stress the importance of honest, but sensitive communication. This is so important in preventing the feeling of resentment later. Keeping a journal to record your feelings can be very helpful during challenging times. Mine became a best friend when my parents were ill. There were many days I knew I had to hold it together and would be anticipating getting into bed with my journal and expressing myself, knowing I would feel better later.

On one occasion, I made a presentation on the topic of keeping your loved one at home and how to best manage this situation. Afterwards, the event organizers had all of the presenters participate in a question and answer panel. The most common question had to do with arguing siblings not being in agreement on how to care for a mother or father in declining health. Whether it was financial, transportation, medical decisions, living arrangements, or the division of care, sibling challenges drove the discussion.

It can be difficult for everyone to agree on every decision, or to even agree on the reality of what is going on with a parent's situation. A common scenario is when an adult child lives out of state and a sibling living close to the parent expresses concern over declining health. The sibling living at a distance may say something like, "I just spoke with Mom the other day, and she sounded fine." This can become frustrating for the adult child who is carrying the responsibility of ensuring a parent's well-being and safety. This is another reason why communication is so essential during the time of decision-making. It is also wise to ask yourself honestly about whether or not you are being a martyr by not accepting help because you think only you know how to do it right. If you keep hearing yourself say, whether silently or aloud, "I always have to do everything," determine if this is really true or have you not tapped into all of your potential resources. If you are really struggling, losing your temper, depressed, or often tearful, reach out for some assistance from a psychotherapist, pastor, or support group. Family caregiving often takes an emotional and physical toll that can have detrimental effects for years to come.

SIGNIFICANT RELATIONSHIPS COUNT

Try to be aware that as difficult as it is for you to be the primary care-giver for your parent(s), your significant relationships are being impacted as well. Chances are you have gradually increased the amount of time you are spending with your mother or father. Your spouse or partner and children may be missing you and don't know how to express it in an appropriate way. They may feel guilty asking you for your time because they realize you are facing major challenges yourself. They may be incredibly angry with you and not realize it. They may be angry with your parent for taking you away from the way things used to be. Their perception may be that they feel neglected, abandoned, and not very important to you. Caregiving impacts everyone directly or indirectly. Giving each person a voice and validating how they may be feeling about the changes is very helpful in resolving difficult situations. When we are heard and understood and feel that we are important to others, we almost always feel better.

Remember your friends, too. Long-term, supportive friendships should not be taken for granted. Now more than ever, nurturing and posi-tive friendships are helpful. I will always be grateful to my friend Debbie for accompanying my dad to an oncology appointment because I was so grief stricken and worn out from hearing bad news that I didn't feel I could handle hearing my dad ask, one more time, another doctor, how long he had to live. I will always remember my friend Cheri making my mom laugh and helping me get her settled when she came to live with me on hospice. I am grateful to my partner who suggested that my mom live with us in the first place. I truly don't know how I would have gotten through these years without the supportive relationships that bolstered me.

Ensure that you take care of all your relationships. People are patient and forgiving, but at a certain point they will become hurt and feel pushed away if you ignore their phone calls and don't respond to emails. If you are really overwhelmed, send a group email to your friends explaining that you are stretched to the limit, but appreciate their understanding and support. Create the time to go for a walk or have lunch with your friends. You want to emerge from this experience with your life and relationships intact.

I'M AN ONLY CHILD

If you are an only child, caring for your aging parent may be more difficult and easier in some respects than if you had siblings. You may feel lonely at times without the support by brothers and sisters. On the other hand, the experience may be less complicated and chaotic than arguing about what is right for your mother or father. Be sure you reach out to friends, seek counseling, or join a support group so you don't isolate yourself during this experience. Many adult children who do have siblings are estranged from them and feel as if they are the only child. However, there is something to be said for having a solid relationship with one or more siblings because you feel that they have an understanding of your parent's and your history. This is what you may feel you are missing. Perhaps you have cousins or aunts and uncles you trust and can connect with to discuss the family circumstances. Maybe you have a childhood friend you can talk to who knew your parents when you were growing up. When our parents are in declining health we tend to reminisce and begin to reflect on our childhoods. It can be comforting to do this with someone who knew you as a child.

RESISTANCE TO ASSISTANCE

Another obstacle families often face is their parents insistence that they do not need any help or assistance of any kind. It is very frightening for a person to feel as if they are losing control over their own lives. When I initially opened my in-home care and assistance agency, eager to help older adults remain in their own homes for as long as possible, I was shocked when the older adult would express that they didn't need any help or want any stranger coming into their home. I would observe their daughters and sons basically slump in their chairs with disappointment as they realized their mom or dad was going to resist help for as long as possible, as this meant no resolution for the stress they were dealing with. This is a time when siblings need to meet and agree on a plan with how to move forward. After doing this with your siblings, sit down with your parent(s) and include them in a discussion about their situation, their changing needs, and your concerns. For as long as they are capable, allow them to have input in the decision-making and show that you value their input. If they feel you are rushing in and taking over, it is more likely you will be met with continued resistance.

Many people become frustrated because they have an unrealistic expectation that their parent will immediately agree with the idea that they need help. Put yourself in their shoes and imagine how this would feel to you. Most people need time to process what is happening and want to feel as if they have control over their own destiny. We especially want to feel control over what we may perceive as our final chapter in life. Older adults don't feel like they have the time or energy to fix the mistake of a decision to sell their home and move into an assisted living facility, for example. Important decisions made at this time of life often feel very final and can feel like the *last stage before the grave*. That is a reality that adult children need to be aware of and respect. Something else to bear in mind is that if you're opposite gender parent needs help bathing and dressing, chances are both of you will not be comfortable if you were to assist them. Even some same gender parents and adult children are simply not comfortable with providing personal care. Your parent's personality traits may be magnified during this time. For example, if they have a very strong, domineering personality, they are more likely to fight you and accuse you of trying to gain control over their life. If this is your situation or if you live at a distance, you may need to explain to your parent that for them to remain in their own home safely, you will both need to come up with some solutions. It may help if you acknowledge that you understand their desire to remain as independent as possible for as long as possible. Ask questions about how they are feeling about their situation; don't assume that you know. Validate their feelings by listening and reflecting back to them what you heard them express.

Ideally, you want to know what is important to your parent(s) as their health declines. Getting an advanced healthcare directive and other important documents in place is important, but it is never too late to deal with the situation; it just may become more challenging the longer you wait. Your parents may indeed become upset with you, but not dealing with the situation can have disastrous results. A time may come when you must step in and make decisions for one or both of your parents in order to avoid financial devastation or physical harm. This is one of the reasons emotional support for you is imperative. Your parent may verbally strike out at you in their frustration over losing control of their health and decision-making capacity. Old wounds may be reopened triggering frequent emotional upsets. Siblings may not be in agreement on how the situation ought to be handled. It can be very helpful to reach out to a trusted friend who has dealt with their own parent's illness and declining health status. If your family isn't able to eventually resolve the conflict, you may want to seek the assistance of a geriatric care manager or family mediator.

COPING WITH DEMENTIA

The early stages of dementia can be a very confusing time for a family. People suffering with the early stages of dementia, act like themselves most of the time, but begin to exhibit uncharacteristic behavior. Family members are often irritated when their mother or father can't remember certain things. A parent may begin to make medication errors or forget appointments. Please be sure your parent is assessed and properly diagnosed. At the same time, educate yourself about their dementia and how it should be handled. You will not be able to "make them remember," or convince them of what reality is. Trying to do so can become an abusive situation for them and extremely futile for you. Do your research and take classes offered to families by the Alzheimer's Association that will help you learn how to communicate and cope with a parent who has dementia. Try to help other family members do the same. Don't be surprised if your brother, sister, or other family members and friends are in denial about the severity of the symptoms. If both of your parents are still living, don't be surprised if your healthy parent covers up for the parent with dementia. They will speak up for them and answer questions and do everything possible to compensate for their partner's memory loss. As you educate yourself, you will learn, for example, that Alzheimer's disease affects the frontal lobe area of the brain. This is the area that regulates our behavior. It is very distressing when a parent behaves in an appropriate manner; such as, undressing, urinating in public, or saying or doing things that could be perceived as threatening.

When a family is adjusting to a diagnosis of some form of dementia, it is extremely stressful and conflict may result. Gather the resources you need as soon as possible so you know where to go for help as the need arises.

WHEN A FAMILY MEMBER IS LGBT

If your parent is gay, lesbian, bi-sexual, or transgender this may complicate things for them emotionally as they need assistance. While homosexuality is becoming more acceptable, it was not considered acceptable in your parent's generation. Many older adults were married for years, had children, and hid their homosexuality from even themselves. They may have serious concerns about others "finding out" about their orientation for fear they will be treated poorly through neglect, ridicule, or even abuse (Morris, 2004). Many older adults who are homosexual and in a facility feel they must go back into the *closet* and hide their history from the staff and other residents. Perhaps they loved the same person for forty years who died, but they never talk about it. They are afraid to talk about the beautiful home they had together, the travel they shared, or their wonderful friends and hobbies. People in facilities often sit in common areas and reminisce about their lives. The homosexual resident may sit quietly because they are afraid to share. This can be the cause of isolation and severe depression. Perhaps you are embarrassed for others to find out your parent is gay, lesbian, or transgender. No person should suffer discrimination for any reason, but it does happen. LGBT education regarding cultural competency for the health profession is increasing, but has a long way to go. There continues to be denial for the need, and even ignorance for the prevalence of homosexuality in the older adult population. Keep in mind, a person's homosexuality is not simply about a "sex act." This descriptive word encompasses within it a person's life history, certain culture and most likely, who they loved and shared life with for a very long time. The label is but one aspect of who they are. Protect your parents and advocate for them. If you have issues with them, reach-out and try to resolve those issues for the sake of your parent's quality of life as they age.

Perhaps you are a part of the LGBT community and have kept this hidden from your parent(s). You may have the added stress and anguish of now spending more time with them and them finding out the "truth." Maybe they need to come and live with you and your partner, and you fear their judgment. You will need to consider the circumstances, their health status, and whether or not you believe telling them would be helpful. You may want to discuss this with a professional so you either reveal the truth in a compassionate manner, or if you choose not to tell, you take care of yourself as the situation with caring for your parent progresses.

MY MOM DIDN'T TAKE CARE OF ME, WHY SHOULD I TAKE CARE OF HER?

This issue is not as uncommon as one might think and can become a moral and ethical dilemma for those faced with this situation. Family members who have possibly been estranged for years are suddenly forced to deal with one another in the interest of helping a parent in need. If the parent(s) were abusive, neglectful or absent altogether, it can be extremely difficult to invest time transporting them to doctor's appointments, grocery shopping, or accompanying them to social events. It is even more emotionally difficult to assist them dressing, using the toilet, bathing, and helping them in and out of bed. One client that I was trying to provide service for didn't raise his children, and they had been marginally estranged for years. He was more like a peer than a father, a distant relative that the children had contact with infrequently. This gentleman's daughter was at a loss when she was contacted because his dementia had become detrimental to his own safety, as well as others. She wanted to want to help, but was resentful and angry at having to put parts of her own life on hold while she tried to ensure her father's safety and well-being.

In addition, adult children in this position are often judged by others as not caring about their parents; this leads to even more guilt and misunderstanding. I faced this many times when I owned my homecare agency and caregivers would pass judgment on the client's adult children for not spending enough time with their parent(s). It was commonplace to have to point out that we were not aware of the context of the situation and did not have an understanding of the family's lack of connection or involvement. It may be valuable for you to seek counseling so you can process your feelings of resentment and hopefully gain some sense of resolution. If at all possible you may want to distance yourself temporarily when painful memories are being triggered and worked out. There are also numerous self-help books available to guide you through this painful time.

To reiterate, when a parent's health is declining and a family is being forced to see one another regularly, emotions often become intense, and at times unmanageable without professional help. Try not to minimize what you are experiencing, it is real and not to be taken lightly.

SHOW ME THE MONEY

Many family arguments, fights, and downright wars occur because of money. When parents haven't planned, prepared, and made decisions about who gets what, this increases the chances of a family having issues over money, property, jewelry, and other possessions. My mom and dad were not wealthy people with an abundance of property and expensive heirlooms to be distributed amongst us. However, they had possessions that were meaningful to my brother and me. My mom began talking about the various items many years before my parent's health began to decline. This made it much easier to have the discussion. She bought small, yellow and blue-colored sticker dots and placed them on the bottom of the items we wished to have. I was blue, my brother yellow. This made it so easy when it came time to divide things up between us. When my mom's father passed away, she and her sister went to war over several issues, including material items and money. This turmoil ended their relationship and they never spoke again. My mom had such a fear this would happen between my brother and I; therefore, she did everything she could do to prevent the same conflict between us.

Arguments over money often occur long before a person dies. For example, an adult child may not want their sibling spending the inheritance they feel entitled to on homecare. Sometimes a sibling moves in with a parent to care for them and other siblings become paranoid that they are stealing mom's money. Sadly, this circumstance does happen, but often the accusations are false. It can't be emphasized enough that keeping the focus on the person being cared for, and doing the right thing for them, is most important. This is another reason why planning and having clear instructions is so helpful. Trying to figure things out while in the midst of a crisis is never recommended. Personal preparedness is just as important as being prepared for an earthquake or knowing where the nearest exits are on an airplane.

MENTAL ILLNESS

If your parent has a history of mental illness, assisting them as they age can be even more difficult and challenging. One client that was cared for by my agency had a long history of being treated for psychiatric problems. Due to the fact that she had been severely physically and verbally abusive to her daughter, her only child, the situation was complicated. She had tripped and broken her neck; as a result, she was a quadriplegic. We took care of her twenty-four-hours-a-day, including bathing, feeding, dressing, turning her every two hours, and much more. Her daughter arranged the care and made sure the bills were paid, but remarked to me one day, "The only reason I speak to my mother is because she's in a chair." The resentment and destruction ran deep between these two women, and it profoundly impacted the mother's situation as her health continued to decline. She had possessed a death wish for many years and pushed every one away who came near her with her vile language and verbal assaults. Even for people who care deeply for others find this type of person difficult to love and provide care for. Much energy may be invested trying to "climb their fences" and break through the barriers they have erected around them. Sooner or later, even the most co-dependent person becomes exhausted, hurt, angry, and gives-up.

If you are in this situation with your parent, ensure that your parent's mental health continues to be addressed along with the physical conditions that may become present. You may need a referral to an appropriate specialist who will monitor medication interactions closely. By all means, seek support to help you cope with the stress and guilt you may be experiencing. Educate yourself about local resources and professionals who can assist you in dealing with the specific manner of your parent's illness. For example, hoarding or compulsive gambling may be how your parent tries to cope with their difficult thoughts and emotions.

FAMILY CONFLICT

It is a reality that some parents play favorites with children and as the family ages, this does not change and causes conflict, making it very difficult to provide shared care for your mother or father. If the arguments are intense and your family situation doesn't improve in spite of efforts to have meetings, make plans, and work together, seek family counseling from a therapist with expertise in this area. You can also hire a geriatric care manager to help mediate and coordinate care for your parent. Family dynamics present themselves in a multitude of ways when a parent's health begins to decline. There are cultural, socioeconomic, geographic and other changeable influences that will impact your specific situation. Educate yourself and seek to understand why your family is behaving the way it is.

If you, a sibling, or your parent is acting out in anger or lack of cooperation, try to discover why. This should be a part of your assessment. You will most likely discover it is one of these reasons:
- Fear of change
- Fear of various losses
  - Health
  - Death
  - Financial

- Independence and autonomy
- Home
- Identity
- Pets
- Privacy
- Fear of parent dying
- Past unresolved emotional pain
- Physical or emotional health problems not properly addressed
  - Pain
  - Difficulty hearing
  - Difficulty seeing
  - Oral health problems
  - Medication interactions and contraindications
  - Incorrect diagnosis
  - Symptoms not thoroughly evaluated
- Fear of being treated unfairly
- Fear of losing inheritance

COMMUNICATION

Honest communication will help your family navigate this often uncertain time. Someone in your family may need to take the lead on making this happen. Remember to keep your parent in mind and do your best to work toward maintaining their quality of life and keeping your life intact. Many people underestimate the impact of caring for an aging parent and are embarrassed to reach out for help. Many families mistakenly believe that only their family behaves this way and don't want anyone to know. While it's true, families are unique; conflict, arguments, and downright personal wars are common during this stage of life. Professionals whom you may seek assistance from see this occurring in families all the time and know how to help. While it's natural to want to protect our families and keep negative behaviors private, try to allow yourself to be vulnerable by reaching out for assistance from empathetic professionals.

"The ache for home lives in all of us, the safe place where we can go and we are and not be questioned."

MAYA ANGELOU

CHAPTER FIVE
Home Sweet Home

*M*y parents were not attached to a home they had lived in for several decades, unlike many older adults. In fact, they enjoyed moving and exploring new neighborhoods. They downsized and moved into a condo long before their health began to decline. Home for my mom and dad was more about the community where they lived. Home, for my mom and dad, was with each other. They wanted to feel familiar with their grocery store, the post office, restaurants, and doctor offices. Waitresses and grocery clerks knew them by name. Once, when my mom was hospitalized, I went out to breakfast with my dad. When my dad left the table to use the restroom, the waitress questioned me, with extreme concern about the whereabouts of my mom. I think moving my mom away from her community was perhaps harder on her than I wanted to believe at the time. She felt out of place and bewildered. My dad, on the other hand, embraced the people he was meeting and otherwise would not have known. I was introducing him to various people for healing purposes. Not to cure his cancer, but to help him feel better and have an improved quality of life for however long he had to live. He remarked to me often about how fortunate he felt to be meeting such wonderful people who were sincere and cared so deeply about helping others.

My mom eventually adjusted to a certain degree. She realized that there was no way I could be visiting her every day if she lived fifty-five miles away. She realized after my dad died that it wouldn't matter where she was; home would never feel like the home she had known with my dad for nearly fifty years. It was important to my mom to never end up in a facility. We accomplished this by adapting to the various issues as they presented themselves. First, we got her a walker, then a shower bench, then a wheelchair, and eventually an oxygen compressor and hospice; all in place to make life at home possible and comfortable.

My mom was taken by ambulance from her apartment one day. Three weeks later she was living with me on hospice, returning only once to her apartment to go through her belongings. This was a heartbreaking time. It was only in retrospect, much later, that I realized just how painful this was for her. I was occupied with my own grief and exhaustion and didn't have the presence of mind to truly address her grief and fears. She felt she had lost her independence, her privacy, and her sacred routines. Losing her privacy was the most difficult, but once again she adjusted, as people do. Most of us do want to age in place (in our own home) and not in a facility; however, this usually means making adjustments; psychologically and to the environment.

"Life is like riding a bicycle. To keep your balance, you must keep moving." Albert Einstein

---

AGING IN PLACE

The Center for Disease Control and Prevention defines aging in place as, "The ability to live in one's own home and community safely, independently, and comfortably, regardless of age, income, or ability level." If your parent's desire is to age in place by remaining in their own home, there may come a time when changes need to be made to make staying home safe and comfortable.

Upon realizing your parent(s) needs a little assistance, you and/or your siblings may begin to visit more often, accompany them to doctor's appointments, begin helping to maintain their home, or begin driving or flying in more often from where you live to check in on them. This type of "care" may expand to visiting more often, doing the grocery shopping for them because it becomes too difficult for them to go out, doing the laundry, the meal preparation, and even stopping by to help them bathe and get dressed. It is common for this scenario to evolve gradually over time; one day you may realize you are completely exhausted, resentful, and neglecting other areas of your own life. It may become necessary to hire an in home care agency, and/or modify your parent's home, so that it is safe and helps them to remain as independent as possible, for as long as possible.

HIRING A FORMAL CAREGIVER: CHOOSING THE RIGHT ONE

You may want to hire a non-medical formal caregiver. Some of the services this person may help your parent with is preparing meals, grocery shopping, light housekeeping, laundry, bathing, assistance with dressing, continence care, feeding, walking, medication reminders, transportation to medical appointments, assistance with transferring and ambulating, monitoring and reporting changes in skin condition, food/fluid intake, socialization, and general companionship. You will want to be sure that the caregiver you hire is familiar with your parent's particular condition. For example, if your mother or father has dementia it will be important that the caregiver be trained and knowledgeable about how this manifests and what they need to do to keep your parent safe and comfortable. Certified Nursing Assistants and Home Health Aides are trained in emptying and caring for catheters or colostomy bags, assisting with rehabilitation activities, and in identifying and reporting signs and symptoms that need attention.

This type of service is most often paid for privately unless the person has a long-term care policy. A few health insurance plans may pay for a very limited number of hours. If your parent is a Medi-CAL (California) or Medicaid beneficiary it is sometimes possible to qualify for "In-Home Supportive Services." If your parent has served in the military you will want to find out if they qualify for veterans benefits. Visit the VA's website listed in the resources section. It is highly recommended that you use a company that performs regular criminal background checks, motor vehicle administration records check, has liability and worker's compensation insurance, is bonded, and directly employs their caregivers, meaning that they are responsible for paying the employee's payroll taxes. In this case, no money is exchanged between the client and caregiver. The employee turns in a signed timecard and you are billed, usually on a weekly basis. In addition, these caregivers are being supervised by the owner of the company or a case manager that is also employed by the company. You may pay a higher hourly fee, but using a bonded and insured agency may save you a lot of grief in the long run.

Most of us have heard at least one horror story of an unwatched caregiver who becomes close to an older adult and takes advantage of the relationship by gaining access to their money and other valuables. Caregivers who become "like family" also are at risk for burnout when they work long hours, feel taken advantage of, and receive no respite because they are the person's sole caregiver. This may put an older adult at risk for emotional and/or physical abuse, as well. When family members live far away or are emotionally estranged from their parent, a vulnerable older adult may feel that if they tell anyone about the abuse they will have no one to care for them, and they will be left to die alone. Again, utilizing the services of a reputable company mitigates the risk of such abuses. This is not to say that it can't happen, but at the very least another set of eyes is watching and any harm intended will hopefully be short lived.

A reputable company will be happy to provide you with proof of insurance and references. Perhaps a local physician's office or rehabilitation center regularly refers patients to the company because they hear wonderful things about them and the high quality caregivers they employ. Ask how they match a caregiver to the client and what happens if your parent isn't comfortable with the caregiver they initially assign to them. Ask about their training and experience and if they are indeed qualified to handle your parent's specific diagnosis. It is perfectly appropriate to request a caregiver that clearly speaks your parent's language and is comfortable preparing food that your parent is familiar with. Most companies keep a journal for the caregivers to write down what occurs during their shift so a supervisor and family members can be informed regularly. Also, ask if the company has a twenty-four-hour answering service, or if the supervisor is on call, in case the caregiver had an emergency and needs someone to cover their shift.

If the caregiver is provided cash to shop for your parent, make sure the receipts and cash are reconciled by either your parent or by you, if your parent is unable to do so. Another option is purchasing a "gift card" that can be reloaded as necessary and request that all receipts be kept.

If the caregiver is going to use their own car for errands and transporting your parent, the company will charge you a per mileage fee. Make sure the company has performed a check of their motor vehicle record and can verify that the employee has insurance and a valid driver's license and vehicle registration. If the caregiver drives the client's vehicle, the client is responsible to insure the vehicle and maintain the car. Mileage reimbursement would not apply in this case.

Don't be surprised if your parent(s) is resistant to this type of care. Most people will state, "I'm fine, I don't need any help." Or, "I don't want a stranger in my home." Suggest that your parent "give it a try" for a few hours a week. For many people, a caregiver being hired to come into the home represents losing control over their daily routine, and ultimately their lives. For example, a private person who is accustomed to getting up in the morning and having their coffee while reading the newspaper, most likely perceives this as sacred time. It can be extremely upsetting to suddenly have someone showing up early in the morning and disrupting a routine that has been in place for many years. For many, it marks a time of no longer being able to care for themselves, which can be depressing. It's important to make sure the caregiver is fostering as much independence as possible. When my mom was living with me and on hospice, it was recommended that we bring in a caregiver because it wasn't safe to leave her home alone for any length of time. In her opinion, it was ridiculous and caused daily arguments between us about why it was necessary for the caregiver to come to the house. One day, while I was busy upstairs, I overheard my mom loudly expressing to the caregiver, "I just want to make myself a sandwich." The caregiver had been following her around wherever she went and she had simply had enough of relinquishing her privacy and independence. My mom was perfectly capable of making her own sandwich. After that incident, we worked out a new plan with the caregiver, who was sincerely just trying to do her job and keep my mom safe.

When an older adult needs help toileting and bathing, two of the most private times in our day, it is imperative that everyone be sensitive to this loss that the person is facing. Care and patience is a must. Whenever possible, the person should be bathed on their usual schedule and not rushed to conform to what the caregiver wants to do. We are all likely to be more pleasant and agreeable when we feel respected and our dignity is protected. It may be helpful if you are present for the first couple of shifts the caregiver has with your parent. This will hopefully put your mind at ease knowing your parent is in good hands and comfortable with their assigned caregiver. If it is truly not a fit, don't be afraid to request a different caregiver. Companies are used to gently handling such issues and would much rather keep everyone happy and retain you as a client. When I owned my homecare company, we always telephoned after the first shift to check in, see how it went, and ask how we could improve our service.

Using the services of a good homecare company often enhances the older adult's quality of life by alleviating the hours of loneliness and possible isolation. When a good match is made, an appropriate friendship often blossoms. This can do a world of good for you as it frees you to focus on your affairs by offering you respite and peace of mind. Remember, at times it is helpful to begin slowly with a few hours of care per week so your parent does not feel as if they are losing control. It is also fine to frame the decision as being possibly a temporary one. You can say, "Mom, when you get stronger and no longer need the help, maybe you won't have to have a caregiver, but for now please give it try." Sometimes parents may fear their children will no longer visit and be a large part of their lives if they bring in the services of a caregiver. They may not even realize they have this fear. Try to reassure your parent that you're not "abandoning" them. You can address it indirectly by saying, "Dad, we won't have the caregiver come on Tuesday because that's our day to go to lunch." You may need to express that you really want the time you spend together to be fun and enjoyable and it seems like it has become task oriented so hiring help will free up that time. Just as children may not be able to express exactly what they are feeling and, as a result, act out in different ways, an older adult, possibly due to a decline in cognitive function or other illness, may not be able to express their concerns and feelings and act out in anger and frustration. Put on your most empathetic hat, and do your best to understand their emotions. We all need to feel like we matter and that our feelings and wishes count, no matter how long we have been living.

Even if your parent is initially resistant to having homecare, it almost always works out, and the person actually ends up enjoying the company and extra support. It can be helpful too to frame the suggestion of hiring caregivers now in order to build a rapport with an agency in case, in the future, there is a crisis, you'll be comfortable and will know where to turn for support. You may want to call it "in home assistance" rather than "caregiving" so as not to imply the loss of independence. I found in my own agency that the wealthier clients, who were already accustomed to hiring help to maintain their homes, had a much easier time of transitioning into "in home care and assistance." A hard working person, who perhaps grew up during the depression and has always done their own cooking, cleaning, and yard work may have a very difficult time with the idea of a stranger coming in and "taking over."

MEDICATION MANAGEMENT

Enough cannot be said for the importance of medication management. If you have become involved in your parent's care, you must become well informed about their medication purposes, frequency, dosage, and possible side effects. In addition, educate yourself about all of the over-the-counter drugs, vitamins, and supplements they take. Make sure you have this list in your parent's "three-ring binder." It is also an excellent idea to keep a copy on your parent's refrigerator and in their wallet; include any drug allergies they may have. Ensure that you, and the primary caregiver, have a copy of the list as well.

Nonmedical caregivers are only allowed to "remind" a person to take their medication. If you have hired a formal caregiver to be with your parent, be sure the medications are set-up properly in a medication box or some type of system that will prevent errors. If your mother or father is experiencing cognitive decline, you will especially need to be aware of how their medications are being administered. Look for changes, missing medication, or running out of drugs too soon or too late. These are all warning signs of improper use.

HOME MODIFICATION AND MONITORING

Home modifications such as: grab bars in bathrooms, special lighting, wheelchair ramps, and safety devices on doors and stoves, may extend the time an older adult needing assistance, is able to remain in their own home. There is also a growing market for what is called assistive technology. Assistive technology (AT) is not just for seniors, but for any person who needs help living independently. These technologies aid in enhancing an individual's quality of life while improving their function. This includes any equipment or system that increases mobility, communication, or environmental control.

When you are doing your parent's in-home assessment, a good place to begin is to consider if your parent(s) needs a telephone with large buttons and volume control beyond a usual telephone. Also, consider a shower chair, raised toilet seat, hearing aids, or magnifying glasses. If your parent's home has stairs, consider if it is still safe for them to be using the stairs.

Many people want to continue using their second floor and don't want to relocate to a one-story home; in this case you may want to discuss getting a stair lift so your parent can get to the second story while mitigating the risk of a terrible fall. You can go online to research whatever it may be that your parent needs for assistance. AT is not just for helping with daily activities and necessities, it is also to help with maintaining the pleasures in life. For example, AT can help with finger dexterity and low vision while playing cards. In addition, there are devices to assist bowlers, golfers, swimmers, and gardeners that eliminate bending and lifting.

When thinking about modifying your parent's home, think about universal design. This refers to a home accommodating the needs of any person with special requirements; for example, the height of sinks and cabinets, the width of a doorway to a bathroom, or the accessibility of the entrance to the home. When making changes to the home, ensure the modifications are done properly. Grab bars installed incorrectly can have disastrous results if they pull out of the wall when your parent tries to put them into use. There are contractors who specialize in these types of home modifications, so do your homework ahead of time.

Another tool for aging-in-place is a medical emergency response system. This would include fire and smoke alarms, protection from someone breaking into the home, and also offers a pendant or watch that a person wears and activates in case of an emergency--a heart attack, stroke, fall, or other medical issue requiring a response for assistance. Some older adults even have video cameras installed in their homes so their adult children, who perhaps live in another state, can monitor remotely from their computer. Health monitoring is another developing tool to help older adults maintain well-being and avoid unnecessary visits to the doctor. For example, data on blood pressure, blood sugar, or weight can be downloaded to a nurse at the doctor's office to determine if any course of action is required. It is becoming very common for patients to communicate and ask health-related questions of their physicians by email. When it becomes an ordeal for a person to leave home and tolerate getting to the doctor, these tools for care, when used appropriately, can be extremely valuable.

If your parent has dementia, special considerations should be made to keep them safe. Many experts state that it's not if a person with dementia will wander, but when. The Alzheimer's Association website has an online store where you can purchase door alarms and other items to help loved ones cope with caregiving for a person with dementia. They also have a nationwide emergency response service for individuals at risk for wandering. This service is a membership program which operates twenty-four-hours-a-day to identify a person as "lost" and alert family members to wandering and medical emergencies. The affected person wears either a pendant or bracelet that contains important medical information. Visit the Alzheimer's Association website (www.alzheimersassocation.org) for accessing their twenty-four-hour-a-day support hotline, schedule of family caregiving classes, and to enroll in their "Medical Alert--Safe Return Program."

ADULT DAY CARE

Adult Day Care Centers are designed to provide care and companionship for seniors who need assistance or supervision during the day. The program offers relief to family members or caregivers and allows them the freedom to go to work, handle personal business, or just relax while knowing their relative is well cared for and safe.

The goals of the programs are to delay or prevent institutionalization by providing alternative care, to enhance self-esteem, and to encourage socialization. There are two types of adult day care: adult social day care and adult day healthcare. Adult social day care provides social activities, meals, recreation, and some health-related services. Adult day healthcare offers more intensive health, therapeutic, and social services for individuals with severe medical problems and those at risk of requiring nursing home care. Costs vary among adult day centers and can range from $25 a day to more than $100 per day depending on the services offered, type of reimbursement, and geographic region. Seniors generally take part in the program on a scheduled basis, and the services that are offered include:

- Education
- Counseling

- Evening care
- Exercise
- Health screening
- Meals
- Medical care
- Medication Management
- Physical therapy
- Recreation
- Respite care
- Socialization
- Supervision
- Transportation

(www.eldercare.gov)

Most families take comfort in knowing they did their best to keep their loved at home for as long as possible. There is often a sense of peace and pride when someone dies in their own home. However, there are situations when it becomes unsafe for all involved when someone in declining health remains at home. Keep this in mind as you go forward. Continue to assess the situation and be willing to make a sensitive, but practical decision if need be.

"Myth: I should always do what others want, expect, or need from me."

HARRIET B. BRAIKER, PH.D.

CHAPTER SIX
Caregiver Stress And Burnout

When my parents moved to be closer to me, I was compelled to prove to them, to my brother, and to myself that this was the right decision. I called several times a day and took a two hour lunch to run their errands and spend time with them. I often stopped by in the evening on my way home from work to make sure everything was truly alright. I gave and gave and kept giving because if I had anything left over at the end of the day, it meant I must not had given enough. I was left with a daunting feeling that I could have done more to improve the situation. Of course, this was not rational, and I completely placed unreasonable and unhealthy expectations on myself. I felt overwhelmingly responsible for my parent's health, their comfort, care, happiness or lack of it. As unhealthy as this was for me, it is not at all uncommon for adult children (usually daughters) to fall into this trap, sometimes completely unaware. In the beginning of my journey, I tried to maintain my regular schedule of working, socializing, and exercising, while adding on my caregiving responsibilities. For me to recharge my batteries I need quiet time alone, and I began having this less and less. The absence of it in my life at that time really took a tremendous toll on me. I justified it by convincing myself that when I was out running, I was alone. While this was true and helpful, it wasn't just quiet time sitting and reflecting, and it wasn't stillness. It was an activity that even though it refreshed my mind and spirit, placed demands on my body. It became another "to do."

When my mom came to live with me during her last five months of life on hospice, I had placed a baby monitor in her room so I could get up and down during the night to assist her with medication and in using the toilet. I think there may have only been a handful of nights that I slept more than two hours straight without bounding out of bed and scurrying down the stairs to help her. My brother paid for her to have a caregiver several hours a day during the week so I could work, but in retrospect I made a grave error by not requesting some sort assistance at night so I could sleep. As a result, I was not functioning at a high level, I was irritable, exhausted, and felt hopeless that my life would get better any time soon. I even had the experience of falling asleep on my feet as I was attempting to have a conversation with one of my mom's doctors. Before that, I didn't realize that this expression was something that could happen in the literal sense. I felt it was my duty and that asking for more help would mean that I didn't care as much as I should. If you have this mindset, it is a dangerous place to be and not good for you or for the one in your care.

I have run several marathons in my life. With the exception of my first one, each time I have trained for the 26.2 mile distance I have been aware of what I was getting myself in to. When my parent's health began to decline to the point where they needed my assistance, I can remember feeling like someone said "run and keep running and there's no telling how far you will need to go." I had no idea of how to pace myself or how long the journey would last. Most of us have the ability to dig deep during difficult circumstances and do what we have to do to get through the situation. When the "difficult circumstances" don't resolve in a reasonable amount of time, severe consequences are often the result.

"Finish every day and be done with it. You have done what you could; some blunders and absurdities no doubt crept in; forget them as soon as you can. Tomorrow is a new day; you shall begin it serenely and with too high a spirit to be encumbered with your old nonsense." Ralph Waldo Emerson

ASLEEP ON MY FEET

Have you ever had the experience of pulling into a gas station only to find that the station itself is out of gas? Have you ever pondered the instructions on the airplane when they tell us to secure our own oxygen mask before we assist others? If you, as a caregiver are running on empty, which is the common scenario, you are not offering your parent(s) the best care possible. Allowing yourself to believe that you have no time to take care of yourself or enjoy simple pleasures could be described as self-defeating behavior. Your life may become slowly consumed by caregiving for your parent until your world shrinks and you become less and less involved with the things that are important to you. Depending upon the reasons for a parent's decline, a caregiving journey may last several years; if you don't take good care of "your life," it may not be there when you return. Your job performance may suffer, you may neglect your marriage and friendships, your children will grow-up, and generally speaking, life will continue to move along while you are sidelined with caregiving tasks. As best you can, allow your caregiving role to blend with your day-to-day life. If at all possible, including your parent in a family dinner once a week, bringing them to your child's sporting event, or allowing your children to participate, in an age-appropriate manner, with the care of your parent can be a rewarding experience for everyone involved. One of the reasons you may be resentful is that you feel as if you have been pulled away from your life and you feel isolated. It is common to feel as if there are simply not enough hours in the day to get done what you "must." A myriad of symptoms, both physical and emotional, may arise and have long-lasting detrimental effects to your health. In addition to taking the time to care for your loved one, you may be worried, grieving, depressed, and anxious. I know I was experiencing all of this, as I attempted to put on a happy face in order to appear as if I was doing just fine. Please look at the signs and symptoms of caregiver burnout and check in honestly with yourself about whether or not you are experiencing any or several of the symptoms.

We live in a twenty-four-hour world. Have you noticed that it doesn't matter what time of the day it is, we are able to be productive? If we can't sleep, we can watch something on television, we can email, or go online and shop or do research. Some stores and restaurants are open twenty-four-hours-a-day. Many of us seem to be on constant alert to accomplish some "thing." Quiet moments of reflection in the darkness are often few and far between. Generally speaking, as a culture, we have come to accept this as normal. In certain circles, if you're not uptight, on edge, rushing around, high energy, or not constantly tapping on your cell phone keys, you risk being perceived as a slacker or lazy. Managing our stress is not simply a luxury, it is essential if we want to live long, healthy, and happy lives. There is no reward at the end of your life for having the most stress, or being the busiest person in town. Most likely, pertaining to a spouse caring for another spouse, various statistics show that approximately 30 percent of caregivers die before the person for which they are providing care. This is attributed to poor health habits and self-neglect by ignoring their own symptoms and not going to the doctor for exams that would catch life-threatening diseases early, when they are curable (*National Alliance for Caregiving in collaboration with AARP; November 2009*).

UNDERSTANDING STRESS

"Toxic Stress"

Hans Selye, an endocrinologist from Canada, called the consistent pattern of changes the body creates in response to the ongoing demands and "stress" of the external environment, **general adaptation syndrome (GAS)** (Kottler & Chen, 2011). What this means for a caregiver who is constantly on duty, or even perceives that they are duty, because they are constantly considering what they need to do next for the care recipient, is that more than 1,000 different chemical responses in the brain are activated to cope with the ongoing stress of the situation.

Stages of General Adaptation Syndrome
Phase 1. Alarm Reaction: The autonomic and endocrine systems set off a series of reactions (fight or flight), including corticosteroids that may weaken the immune system.
Phase 2. Resistance: The constant stress will activate resistance with the purpose to sustain life and adapt by making "fuel" available for as long as necessary. Eventually, the body becomes depleted and will run out of fuel. Compare this to firing a gun over and over until it runs out of ammunition.
Phase 3. Exhaustion: If the stress remains in place (real or imagined), exhaustion will take over, resulting in permanent damage, illness, or even death.

(Kottler & Chen, 2011)

Following is a list of the most common physical and emotional symptoms that result from general adaptation syndrome. Think of them as lights activating in an emergency notification system, such as the one in the dashboard of your car: fuel level low, oil level low, time for service, check your tires, etc. Do you care enough about your car to stop, pay attention, and address the issue? Please, care enough about yourself and your loved ones to do the same when you exhibit these signs of stress.

PHYSICAL SIGNS OF STRESS

- Problems sleeping or staying asleep
- Back, shoulder, or neck pain
- Digestive issues
- Weight gain or loss
- Eating disorders
- Hair loss
- Fatigue
- High blood pressure
- Shortness of breath
- Cold hands or feet
- Skin problems (itching, eczema, psoriasis, hives)
- More colds, flu than usual

EMOTIONAL SIGNS OF STRESS

- Anxiety
- Depression
- Irritability
- Lack of concentration
- Substance abuse
- Phobias
- Overreactions
- Conflicts at work
- Increased arguing
- Social isolation
- Road rage
- Domestic violence

One of my dear friends, the oldest of three daughters, began to feel overwhelmed with the duties and decisions involved with caring for her eighty-year-old father who had Parkinson's disease and dementia. She quickly realized that she needed to call a meeting with her two sisters and express to them that they really needed to divide the duties with her and asked them how, not if, they could help. They divided up the days and duties and one of the most touching parts of their situation was that they included, whenever possible, their father in the activities of the three grandchildren. Their entire situation was transformed from resentment to cooperation, as the one sister even planned a family dinner each Sunday that included their father. This proved to be an immensely important time for all involved as their father did not live as long as they had hoped. One activity that lit up their father's life was attending his oldest grandson's football games. As a former football player himself, he and his grandson bonded even more, and the joy he felt when watching the games was well worth the extra effort it took to get him to the field. Ultimately, it was necessary for the family to place their father in an assisted living facility due to the safety issues of him living at home alone. Bringing a caregiver into the home was another option, but he refused, and the family decided together on the option of an assisted living facility. They continued to include their father in family outings and dinners after he relocated, but at the same time, they knew when he was "home," he was safe. This alleviated much of the burden of worrying constantly if he was okay or not.

Had my friend not acted proactively to communicate with her siblings, she could easily have found her own sense of well-being at risk. In addition, primary caregivers may find themselves self-medicating by drinking alcohol in excess and/or taking legal or illegal drugs to take the edge off, remedy anxiety, or to help them sleep.

It is possible to travel this journey and remain balanced at the same time. This is not to say that you will not feel any discomfort, sadness, or other difficult emotions, but you can learn how to center yourself and get as much out of the journey as possible.

WHAT CAN YOU DO?

ARE YOU A CONTROL FREAK? BE HONEST . . .

"Only I know how to do this right." Do you hear yourself saying that in your mind? As my caregiving time went on with my parents, I came to believe, not only that only I knew best, but that others weren't even capable of learning about the medicines, the timing of the inhalers, or how to work the oxygen compressor. It's very easy to become obsessed with your parent's care and feel responsible for every moment of their lives. If you are to get through this, without serious consequences to your physical and emotional health, you must be reasonable and realize you simply can't do this alone. Chances are you can "teach" your family members how to administer the necessary medications to your parent, for example. You can also take the time to show them where things are and explain your parent's limitations, as well as their strengths and capabilities. This is another reason why having a notebook that includes the important "plan of care" information is so helpful. They may not perform their duties exactly as you would, but as long as they keep your parent safe from harm, try to allow that to be okay. Consider that they may even have some wonderful suggestions you may find valuable and useful. In addition, your parent may enjoy having a new face around for a change. It may refresh, what ideally ought to be, your *care partnership.*

Giving others a chance to help may enrich their lives, as well. I have a very meaningful memory of calling my dearest friend, Cheri to assist me with washing my mom's hair. My mom had been brought home from the hospital in an ambulance, expected to live only days. One morning she asked me, "Am I dying?" I wasn't sure how to answer; so I replied, "What do you think mom, are you?" She then told me she wasn't ready. I knew, at that point in time, I needed to help her live, not die. She desperately wanted her hair washed, but was too weak to rise from bed. Cheri came over to help me use a bucket to wash my mom's hair while she remained in bed. Cheri had somewhat known my parents over the years and had been an incredible support to me and my family when my dad was dying. After my dad died, Cheri and my mom developed a very endearing friendship. Cheri still often expresses to me that she wished she had known my mom sooner. The friendship was a gift to both of them and to me because I got to witness the tenderness and humor between the two. Helping others through actions or support is rewarding for most of us. Give others a chance to show your parents and you that they care. Cheri loves Christmas. After my mom died, I gave her my mom's artificial poinsettias (lots of them). Cheri arranges them in her entry way planter, along with many lights and other decorations. Each year, I am touched as I approach her home and see the bright red poinsettias welcoming me; a symbol of their friendship and the connection made at the end of my mom's life.

CAREGIVING AND CO-DEPENDENCE

"I SHOULD BE ABLE TO DO IT ALL"

If you are co-dependent, it may be true to say that you have been "overdoing" for others most of your life. Most likely, the way you feel good about yourself and the way you "feed" your self-esteem is gauged by how much you do for other people. Harriet Braiker, in her book *The Disease To Please,* suggests taking an inventory and selecting tasks to delegate. She recommends going through your appointment book and making a list of all the tasks, projects, jobs, and chores you perform and how often you do them. Make sure your list includes the things you do for yourself as well as for others. After you have done this, select a minimum of 10 percent of the chores to delegate to someone else. For example, if you do thirty things, delegate three of them to another. Braiker reminds us that we are "intrinsically valuable human beings and amount to far more than the sum of things we do for others" (2001, p. 215). If you know you are co-dependent, or even suspect that you may be, I highly recommend this book. If you sincerely read it thoroughly and follow the exercises, it can set you free. When I find myself falling back into the patterns of co-dependence, I pick up this book and read the appropriate sections again. Many caregivers have a pattern of trying to *please and fix,* in an endless attempt to make up for what is falsely perceived as their own insignificance.

If you are to emerge from your caregiving experience with your personal and professional lives intact, you will need to delegate tasks. When someone offers to help you, don't simply say, "Thank you, I'll let you know." Instead, think about how they could best assist you and ask them when they are available. Create a schedule to specify who does what and when.

"IT'S MY TURN TO CARE FOR THEM"

Many of us feel that since our parents cared for us when we were young, it's our turn to care for them as they age. This reciprocity, especially in certain cultures, is a given in many families. However, bear in mind that even the most attentive and nurturing parents are not with their children twenty-four-hours-a-day. Parents, unless of course their child is disabled in some way, watch and marvel at the growth and advancements their children make as they become more and more independent. When we are caring for a parent in declining health, we are often grieving the losses and not celebrating the gains. Often, they are becoming more dependent rather than independent. I hope you will keep this in mind if you are feeling guilty about sharing caregiving responsibilities. If you are an only child, be creative and look to your community for resources that can offer you respite.

A caregiver who is burned out is at risk for abusing their parent, not just physically, but verbally and emotionally, as well. You may find yourself saying cruel things to your parent or squeezing their arm so tight they bruise. You may neglect them by leaving them alone for hours and hours without proper nutrition and hydration. Sadly, one of my burned out "caregiving" massage clients admitted to dumping a glass of cold water over her mother's head because she couldn't remember what day it was. It wasn't even a confession of guilt to me; she felt her mother deserved it. She desperately wanted to do it all and *make* her mother better, but found herself becoming more and more angry and irritable. As a result, she became an "elder abuser," not a caregiver. Keep yourself in check so this doesn't happen in your family.

CAREGIVER'S BILL OF RIGHTS

I HAVE THE RIGHT:
- To take care of my own health, spirit, and relationships.
- To seek help from others even though my care-receiver may object.
- To accessible and culturally appropriate services to aid in caring for my care-receiver.
- To get angry and express other difficult feelings occasionally.
- To accept help that is offered to me by others.
- To receive consideration, affection, forgiveness, and acceptance for what I achieve as a caregiver.
- To take pride in what I accomplish and to applaud the courage it has sometimes taken to meet the needs of my relative, partner, or friend.
- To protect my individuality and the right to make a life for myself that will sustain me in the time when my care-receiver no longer needs my full-time help.
- To expect and demand increased awareness and support to find resources to aid me in caring for my relative, partner, or friend.

Author Unknown

TOOLS FOR SURVIVAL
- Exercise 30 minutes, 3 times per week minimum: Walking, running, dancing, yoga, work out at the gym, bicycling, playing a sport—whatever it is that brings you joy. Regular exercise builds confidence, boosts energy levels and stamina. It also releases the "feel good" hormones in our brains.
- Eat healthy/drink water: Avoid junk food and soda, eat plenty of fresh vegetables and fruits. Drink half of your weight in ounces of water per day. Example: If you weigh 140 lbs, drink 70 ounces of water per day.

- Get a massage: If money is tight, check with a local massage school--they offer discounts to the public in order for students to receive practice hours. Don't assume it won't be a quality massage–these are excited and inspired students who aren't burned out.
- Listen to music: Something soothing to you or music from a time in your life when you were happy and carefree.
- Take long, hot baths: Use healing salts or aromatherapy, light a candle, and breathe deeply.
- Meditate and/or pray: Spend quiet time reflecting deep within your heart and listening for messages of wisdom and hope.
- Sleep 7-8 hours every night: This will make you a better caregiver and keep you sane. The body and mind cannot operate properly when it is sleep deprived.
- See friends for fun and support: Don't feel guilty about playing or having fun–it will give you an energy boost to be a better caregiver.
- Seek counseling: Talking about your situation with a trusted professional in a setting that is confidential can help. Make sure you interview several therapists to ensure a good match with your personality and circumstances. No one is an expert on everything.
- All feelings are temporary: Keep the faith that even the most difficult of situations and emotions will pass. Remember the saying, "It's always darkest just before the dawn."
- Remember to laugh: Watch a funny show, movie, or go see a live performance by a comedian. Laughter releases "feel-good" chemicals in the brain.

"Teahouse Practice" means that you don't explicitly talk about "Zen." It refers to leading your life as if you were an old woman who has a teahouse by the side of the road. Nobody knows why they like to go there. They just feel good drinking her tea. She's not known as a Buddhist teacher She doesn't say, "This is a Zen Teahouse." All she does is simply serve tea. No one knows about her faithful attention to the practice, it's just there in the serving of the tea, her attentiveness, and the way she cleans the counters and washes the cups."

ANONYMOUS

CHAPTER SEVEN
The Art Of Zen Caregiving

Teahouse practice describes a Zen approach to not just serving customers tea, but how you live your life. Zen is the practice (the art) of being present for every moment of your life. It's not *what* you are doing, but *how* you are doing it. Whether you are aware of it or not, being calm and present makes a tremendous difference in the outcome of caregiving situations. Have you ever been in a wonderful restaurant where you feel good just being there? The environment is calm and quiet, and you know the chef absolutely loves what he or she does for a living: all of this "good energy" comes through in the food as you ingest it. In contrast, have you ever had a massage from someone who is rushing as they slap oil on you? You can "feel" whether or not the person is present and enjoying the moment; it comes through their hands. The same is true when we are caregiving for a loved one. This is another reason to take care of yourself and handle any potential burnout. This approach does not deny or gloss over the fact that caregiving can be extremely stressful and even painful at times, but encourages a caregiver to face those issues and clear them out in order to open the space to truly "care" and allow the love to flow through you. If you can manage to be in the moment and remain present for each task you are performing, the experience will not only be better for the care recipient, but much more rewarding for you as well; it is then truly, a care partnership.

TOUCH MATTERS

Sometimes it can be difficult to hold out hope that a situation will improve, but try not to give up. When my dad was informed he was terminally ill and all the medical community could do for him was keep him comfortable with medications, it was nearly impossible to feel hopeful. However, because he was open to trying new, non-traditional modalities, not to cure his lung cancer, but to enhance the quality of his life, he had experiences and made wonderful connections with people that he never dreamed possible. I could share the individual stories here, but I think what sums it up best is to simply say that he felt better because he felt loved and cared about. Technically, he was dying, but he was more alive than he had been in years because he was surrounded with support. He was expressing himself, and he was accepting of his journey with an open heart.

I provided massage, Reiki, Bach Flower remedies, and guided meditation for my mom and dad. My dad willingly went to acupuncture, infusion therapy, and took numerous supplements to enhance his immune system. We had a psychotherapist come to my parent's home to talk about the situation, the changes, and the grief that was present. He met loving and caring people who made an enormous difference in his end-of-life experience. Our entire family felt stronger and more loved as a result of the support we were receiving. Historically, we were private, even secretive about our challenges, but we knew in this situation we needed help.

For many years I had an office near an "independent retirement community" where I practiced massage, healing bodywork, guided meditation, and taught classes on self-healing and meditation to reduce stress and cope with chronic disease and life-threatening illness. Initially, I was surprised by the great number of "seniors" from the nearby community who were interested in my services and classes. Over time, I have realized that my interest in how we age: physically, emotionally, mentally, and spiritually-- began with my connections to many of these wise people. Many were thoughtful and deep-thinking people who were already practiced in the art of caring for their body and soul. Others struggled with addictions and habits that had taken a toll on their bodies as the years had passed.

What everyone had in common, no matter their age, was the search for happiness and to feel loved. I will never forget a special gentleman, in his late seventies, who scheduled a massage with me during my first month in the business. He had been in a minor car accident and his chiropractor referred him to me to help with his muscle soreness and stiffness. I rubbed massage lotion onto my hands and as I applied the first strokes up his back he began to cry. I asked him if he was alright and he replied, "No one has touched me in about twenty years, thank you." During that hour he shared his stories of the war, losing his wife, and not seeing his adult children and grandchildren very often. Many of us are aware of the need humans have for touch and care, but too often it is forgotten as we age. Remember, multiple losses- spouse, partner, friends, pets-- often results in a person shutting down physically and emotionally. People of any age need to feel loved by others or they may give up on their own health; making it difficult to find a reason to live.

HOLISTIC CARE FOR YOU AND YOUR PARENT

Holistic Treatment: "Considering all aspects of a person's needs and experiences-- physical, emotional, mental, spiritual"

COMPLEMENTARY AND ALTERNATIVE MEDICINE (CAM)

There are many terms used to describe approaches to healthcare that are outside the realm of conventional medicine as practiced in the United States. The National Center for Complementary and Alternative Medicine (NCCAM) explains some of the terms used related to CAM. Perhaps you are well acquainted with phrases such as: healthy aging, productive aging, successful aging, positive aging, or active aging. You may have your own ideas about exactly what this means, but I think we can all agree that the phrases infer a pleasant experience of aging. This doesn't mean an aging experience without challenges, wrinkles, or aches and pains, but it does mean the person is engaged as fully as possible with their own life's journey. We live in a time of having many resources available to assist us in remaining as healthy and comfortable as possible for as long as possible. While it is true that many of these resources must be paid for privately, an older adult can often find some reasonable fees through senior centers or businesses that offer "senior discounts" (http://www.nccam.nih.gov).

Don't assume that your parent(s) would not be interested in a yoga class, a meditation or prayer group, or massage therapy. They may not be aware of what's available in their community; ask them if they would like you to explore some options. It's never too late to have an enriching experience. As I mentioned, my dad had only months to live, but enjoyed massage therapy, acupuncture, homeopathy, meditation, and Reiki. I think it's important to remember that the gift goes both ways and those providing services to older adults usually find their work extremely rewarding. If your parent enjoys the services and feels fulfilled, this may help you to feel as if you're not carrying the burden alone.

These modalities can also be a tremendous benefit to you as you navigate the often turbulent waters of caregiving. Consider making it an outing for you both. In addition, many practitioners will make house calls. As we age, much time is spent talking about ailments, aches and pains, prognosis, medicine, and procedures. We often become hyper-focused on all that is "wrong" physically. Reminding ourselves that our lives are meant to be about much more than that can be very beneficial to our overall health.

I prefer to calls these modalities "tools for empowerment" because they assist by guiding us to be proactive and not victims of our circumstances. Many can be done in an affordable way or even for no charge (breathing, for example). Consider these tools for you and your parent.

Look to this day, for it is life, the very life of life.
In its brief course lie all the realities and verities of
existence.
The bliss of growth, the splendor of action, the glory
of power.
And yesterday is but a dream, and tomorrow is only
a vision.
But today - well lived - makes every yesterday
a dream of happiness,
and every tomorrow a vision of hope.
Look well, therefore, to this day.
~ Sanskrit proverb ~

Physical ~Emotional ~Mental~ Spiritual (PEMS) - Holistic modal-ities address these four dimensions of being. The intention is to restore balance and wellness on all levels.

Physical - Our bodies respond to different thoughts and emotions. The chemical processes in our bodies change depending on which types of emotions we are feeling. Perhaps you are already familiar with this explanation of health or it may sound like nonsense to you. Nevertheless, countless studies have been done that show a correlation between positive thinking and a healthy body. I think we can all agree that heart attacks and strokes are related to stress. When a person thinks about pleasure and feels hopeful about life, the body shifts into a relaxed state where certain chemical changes result and healing can occur. When a person is angry, different chemical reactions occur in the body and create stress on various organs, especially the liver and pancreas. If these emotions continue for extended periods of time, illness can result.

Western medicine has changed tremendously through the years and is beginning to accept and address the fact that a person's emotional state directly impacts their overall physical health. It is becoming more common, depending upon where you live, to find traditional medicine housed under the same roof with CAM.

Emotional - There are two basic underlying emotions in all human beings with varying degrees of intensity-- love and fear. Desire, joy, pleasure, contentment, acceptance, hope, peacefulness, excitement, self-esteem, assertiveness, and generosity are a few examples of love-based feelings. Anxiety, anger, guilt, sorrow, apathy, bitterness, jealousy, irritability, depression, rejection, pity, aggressiveness, powerlessness, passiveness, and loneliness are examples of fear-based emotions. Different chemicals are produced by our bodies when we feel these two groups of emotions.

Repressed feelings don't just go away. They can distort a person's present behavior and create illness and "dis-ease" in the body. When a person doesn't deal directly and honestly with themselves and their emotions they eventually become so disconnected from themselves that they are no longer present to themselves, or to anyone else. Many books have been written in the past several years concerning the direct effect emotions have on our health. Emotions are the direct cause of all illness in our bodies. Authors such as Deepak Chopra, Louise Hay, Barbara Ann Brennan, David Roeland, and so many others have all written wonderfully on this topic. If this resonates for you, I strongly encourage you to read these authors to fully understand the breadth and depth that our emotions impact our physical health.

Mental - The mind/brain stores, organizes, retrieves, and analyzes pieces of information. Western culture tends to be "head-centered," using mind/brain-centered functions as the means to solve problems, collect information, analyze information, and make decisions based on this analysis. The mind/brain used in this manner is an incomplete tool. It does not include the intuition or deep intention that is contained in every human being. It does not include that moment of *knowing*, when we just know something, or that moment of inspiration. How often do we ask ourselves, after having completed a mind/brain analysis, "What does my heart say?" It often says something completely different from our mind/brain conclusion. Has anyone ever said to you, "Follow your gut, it never lies?" This is because we are equipped with an intuitive information system available to guide us for all sorts of reasons. Often, we simply don't listen.

The mind and emotions are constantly responding to the condition of the physical body and the physical body is constantly responding to the meanings and perceptions of the mind and the emotions. This is why, when dealing with illness and the health of the mind, our emotions and body must be dealt with in an integrated manner for wholeness to be present.

SPIRITUALITY

"You cannot find peace by avoiding life." Virginia Woolf

Many individuals confuse organized religions and spirituality. Organized religions are groupings of individuals who usually have a defined set of doctrines or beliefs along with regular practices of worship. Spirituality is the practice of love-based attitudes which are integrated into an individual's everyday life. Spirituality is practiced by the individual. These attitudes and practices can be shared with others, but do not require an organized grouping for their practice.

Worshipping can be very simple and can be done alone or with others. There are many practices which can be used as forms of worship in living a spiritual life. Some people pray to God, Jesus, Allah, Buddha, or whomever they feel a connection. Others meditate, daydream, walk in nature, hike, or go for a run or bike ride amongst the trees on the dirt trails. Some people quiet their minds and connect with Spirit by burning candles, incense, or sage to dissolve negative energies and purify their surroundings and themselves. Others face Mecca and say special prayers five times each day. Some fast during certain periods of the year. Some chant and others sing. There are so many ways to worship and each has its own special beauty (Mary Kurus - www.mkprojects.com).

TAKING CARE OF BODY, MIND, AND SPIRIT

Massage and Bodywork - There's no denying the power of bodywork. Regardless of how we describe the experience (pampering, rejuvenating, or therapeutic), or the reasons we seek it out (a luxurious treat, stress relief, pain management), massage therapy can be a powerful tool for managing uncomfortable symptoms and fostering a sense of well-being.

If your budget allows, massage therapy can be a valuable modality for relieving stress and nurturing yourself. Other forms of healing, such as Reiki, TouchTherapy, cranio-sacral therapy, Trager Therapy can be extremely powerful in escorting us through challenging times. Sometimes we are afraid to fully acknowledge our pain and as a result, we dance around it trying to avoid feeling it. We may fool ourselves into thinking we're not hurting, but the energy of the pain will leak out and express itself in various ways such as anger, sadness, overeating, not eating enough, medicating ourselves, etc. Very often we are not even sure what we are feeling. It's that sense of feeling like something isn't right, but we can't quite put our finger on it. We can't quite "get in touch with what we are truly feeling." This is why bodywork and psychotherapy, can both be valuable tools because they help to move the stuck "clutter" around so we can gain clarity, and ultimately free ourselves to experience more positive emotions. During difficult times it can be helpful to reach out to another and have a seasoned companion help us navigate the rough waters of our journey. In order to think clearly we need to feel safe enough to let our defenses down and get in touch with a healthier reality.

As I have mentioned, family caregiving can be extremely overwhelming when dormant issues reveal their ugly heads and unleash family pain that may have been neatly tucked away for years. Whether the issues involve parents, siblings, or both, the situations that may arise can test our very core. If you try to muddle through, you may pay for it later through severe physical and/or emotional consequences. Choose a modality that feels comfortable for you, and if possible, try to get a referral for a practitioner. Interview the person on the phone and explain what you are presently going through. Follow your intuition as to whether or not you feel a level of comfort and safety with the person.

Geriatric Massage Therapy – This type of bodywork is designed to address the specific needs of the older adult population. Geriatric massage is for more vulnerable or frail adults and uses gentle and light application of massage techniques. This may include passive stretching and a light oil or lotion to permit the muscles to be worked without causing excessive friction to the skin. These techniques can help enhance blood circulation, manage depression, improve balance and flexibility, reduce the pain of arthritis, increase joint mobility, improve posture, and increase a person's overall sense of well-being. A person who is properly trained will want to know your parent's health status and conditions so they do not cause injury. In addition, they will be able to assist your parent in getting on and off the massage table safely and know how to bolster them with supportive pillows when they are on the table.

Senior Fitness Classes and Physical Therapy – Balance, mobility, flexibility, and strength can be improved, even in a frail adult. Don't make the mistake of assuming your parent's condition or quality of life can't be improved upon. Ask their physician for a referral for physical therapy and check within their community for senior fitness classes. "Not being able to manage the activities of daily living is one of the most common reasons people enter nursing homes. Physical frailty is often what keeps people from these activities and robs them of their independence" (National Institutes of Health, 2012). We are all used to hearing about the importance of physical fitness, regardless of our age. However, for older adults, the key function of fitness is to maintain functional mobility and independence (Rikli & Jones, 2013). In addition, older adults who participate in some type of fitness program often benefit socially by making friends who support and encourage them on a regular basis.

Acupuncture - According to the World Health Organization (WHO), acupuncture is effective for treating twenty-eight conditions, while evidence indicates it may have an effective therapeutic value for many more. People with tension headaches and/or migraines may find acupuncture to be very effective in alleviating their symptoms, according to a study conducted at the Technical University of Munich, Germany. Another study at The University of Texas M. D. Anderson Cancer Center found that twice weekly acupuncture treatments relieved debilitating symptoms of xerostomia (severe dry mouth) among patients treated with radiation for head and neck cancer. Many people report that acupuncture has been helpful in relieving their arthritis pain, allergies and other sinus issues, back pain, shoulder pain, digestive problems, and many other conditions.

In Chinese medicine, stress, anxiety, depression, or any strong emotion interrupts the smooth flow of energy throughout the body. According to Chinese medical theory, energy flows through our body through a network of "roads," almost like a highway system. Stress, anger, or any intense emotion acts like a traffic jam, blocking the free flow of energy in the body. For example, many people who are very stressed complain of upper back, shoulder, and neck pain. This is because stress is causing tension in those areas, blocking the free flow of energy, causing pain, tightness, and often leading to headaches. From a Western viewpoint, acupuncture works to alleviate stress by releasing natural pain-killing chemicals in the brain, called endorphins. In addition, acupuncture improves circulation of blood throughout the body, which oxygenates the tissues and cycles out cortisol and other waste chemicals. The calming nature of acupuncture also decreases heart rate, lowers blood pressure, and relaxes the muscles.

Chiropractic Care – Some may feel frightened at the thought of an eight-two-year-old having her neck twisted to adjust her cervical spine; however, chiropractic care can benefit most people. A qualified Doctor of Chiropractic (DC) knows how to treat older adults safely. Chiropractic care has been shown to reduce pain, increase flexibility and mobility, help with balance and help people sleep. A good chiropractor does much more than "crack a person's bones." They work with the soft tissues of the body (muscles, tendons, and ligaments), balance, mobility, and flexibility. They often provide ultrasound and other forms of physical therapy to treat conditions and improve functional ability.

Meditation/Prayer – The intention of meditation is to focus one's attention on various objects or scenes. It could be a focus on sensations of breathing, emotions or thoughts, or observing any type of body sensations. It's about bringing the mind back to the here and now, as opposed to letting the mind wander and worry. Many people express that they have difficulty meditating because they don't have time or they can't stop their minds from wandering. A wandering, busy mind is part of the human condition in varying degrees. The purpose of meditation is to tame your thoughts and calm your mind. It takes continued practice to be "successful," however; we can also try too hard and become frustrated. In meditation, we are allowing ourselves to simply be and not do. Develop a habit of meditating before or after you journal. It is best to meditate with a straight spine, but feel free to sit in a comfortable chair to attain this posture. Free yourself from distractions, such as the telephone, TV, etc. You may find it helpful to play meditative music or even use a guided meditation, especially in the beginning of your practice. Lighting a candle or creating mood lighting is also helpful in inducing a relaxed state of mind.

One of the easiest ways to meditate is by focusing on your in and out breath. Simply become aware of breathing in and breathing out. Green is known as a very calming color; as a result, you may want to visualize filling your lungs with the color green on the inhale and letting go of all stress on the exhale. As you relax you will hopefully arrive in a place of no-thing-ness. In other words, you are no longer holding on to worries and other "things" that prevent you from enjoying the present moment.

I find the most powerful way to pray is to empty my heart and mind by expressing myself, my worries and concerns to our Creator, the loving presence that is everywhere and within every living thing. Upon feeling complete, I listen with a sincere and open heart. When I enter this state of being with pure intentions, I am never disappointed, but I am filled with a deep wisdom and inner peace. The action, if any, I need to take in the particular situation becomes clear. Time spent in silence reveals our soul to us and calms us down. The outside world is constantly distracting us and luring us into feeling stressed. So does dwelling on the past and worrying about the future. Meditation and prayer can help us come home to ourselves. When we are centered and feel that inner harmony, any situation we are faced with becomes easier. We respond in strength and peacefulness, rather than reacting from a place of feeling threatened and in pain.

Yoga – Practiced for thousands of years in the East, yoga is a way of life that includes physical and mental exercises intended to foster spiritual enlightenment. In the West, it is mainly used as a modality for fitness, reducing stress, and preventing illness. There are many styles of yoga, ranging from the very gentle hatha yoga to the more vigorous, astanga yoga. Interview the yoga instructor before beginning a class to learn of their specific orientation and focus. There are classes designed to meet the needs of older adults or those with various challenges.

Tai Chi – This is a Chinese martial art which involves slow, synchronized movements that address the body and the mind. Tai Chi has become quite popular for older adults in recent years. While its practice is beneficial for all ages, Tai Chi has been shown to improve posture, balance, reduce falls, alleviate depression, lower blood pressure, and even increase independence (Morris, 1996). Tai Chi is not a "work out," but instead, is a "work in." It can feel incredibly empowering, calming and centering.

Psychotherapy - Psychotherapy for geriatric issues can help older adults who may have difficulty with the transitions of aging to manage their emotions, find new sources of enjoyment and meaning, and find new support systems. It can help people face their fears of death and deal with grief over the passing of friends and family. It can also assist you as a caregiver by helping you cope with emotions, communication issues (especially likely if a parent has some form of dementia), and link you to community resources. Be sure to interview the therapist to confirm their area of interest and specialty. When our parent's health is failing and we immersed in family issues, it can be a time of reliving our childhoods in a profound manner. While this may be painful for some, remember it can also be a time that offers you the opportunity to resolve issues and free you to discover the person you truly are.

Guided Imagery - Over the past 25 years research findings increasingly demonstrate the effectiveness of guided imagery on health, creativity, and performance. Guided imagery is a program of directed thoughts and suggestions that guide your imagination toward a relaxed, focused state. You can use an intstructor, recordings, or scripts to help facilitate the process. Studies reveal that in many instances, even ten minutes of imagery can reduce blood pressure, lower cholesterol and glucose levels in the blood, and heighten short-term immune cell activity. It can considerably reduce blood loss during surgery and morphine use afterwards. It lessens headaches and pain. It can increase skill at skiing, skating, tennis, writing, acting, and singing; it accelerates weight loss and reduces anxiety; and it has been shown, again and again, to reduce the aversive effects of chemotherapy, especially nausea, depression, and fatigue (www.healthjourneys.com).

Guided Autobiography – Have you noticed that older adults like to reminisce? Telling stories about the history of our lives can be very therapeutic. Writing about our lives and sharing offers us meaning. For an older adult, sharing their life story with others can be immensely enriching. Guided autobiography, also called life review, reminiscence, or memories is conducted in a variety of settings from a small or large workshop to one on one. The "leader" introduces a theme and allows time for reflection before the person shares their story. Most people emerge surprised with the depth and wonder of their story. Search online for a professional in your area who works with older adults and provides guidance for this wonderful process (Birren & Cochran, 2001).

Bach Flower Remedies - Developed by Dr. Edward Bach (1886 - 1936), a Harley Street Clinic physician and prominent bacteriologist, homeopath, and researcher. Dr. Bach believed that mental attitude plays a vital role in maintaining health and recovering from illness. After leaving London in 1930, Dr. Bach explored the English countryside for several years in search of plant-based remedies. In 1934, he decided to settle down and create a center for his work, choosing for its location Mount Vernon, a small cottage in Sotwell, Oxfordshire. He spent the last years of his life at Mount Vernon, where he completed his research. Today, Mount Vernon is better known as the Bach Centre, and its present custodians continue to prepare the mother tinctures, or the first process in making the Bach remedies, often using plants from the same locales that Dr. Bach identified in the 1930s.

Bach flower remedies target the mental/emotional state of an individual, helping to clear negative emotions, mindsets, attitudes, and personality traits that not only impede the body's ability to heal itself, but also creates roadblocks to inner peace and happiness. Bach remedies are useful in dealing with stress, fear and anxiety, depression, anger and resentment, excessive worry, low self-esteem, guilt, and loneliness.

There are other companies that make wonderful flower essences that you may want to explore. I am most familiar with the Bach Remedies and have used them for years with amazing results. My mother, who was very skeptical of many "alternative" modalities, simply swore by the effectiveness of these remedies. When her remedy bottle was only half empty she would ask me to get her more because she didn't want to run out. In case you are wondering, they are not addictive in any way. They just work in a very subtle, but powerful way. They can truly "ease the way" through difficult times of stress. You can find them at your local health food store. Accompanying the remedies will be a questionnaire to guide you to the appropriate remedy for what you are currently feeling.

Reiki – Translated into English, Reiki means, "spiritually guided life-force energy." It can be a complement to anyone's religion or absence of religious belief. Reiki has been included as part of the wisdom of many cultures since ancient times. A treatment feels like a loving, warm-flowing stream of energy (Love) that invokes a sense of peace, security, and well-being on all levels. The practitioner will place their hands on or just above your clothed body as you relax, breathe, and perhaps meditate, pray, or simply do nothing at all.

Sleep Hygiene - Most of us are aware of the importance of getting a good night's sleep, and it does indeed provide us with many positive results.

Some of the possible and well documented consequences of not getting enough sleep are lack of ability to think clearly, irritability, depression, slow reactions, inability to cope with stressful situations, and impaired immune function. Practicing what has been mentioned in this chapter: exercise, good nutrition, meditation, journaling, bodywork, and acknowledging our negative states of mind -- can all assist us in being able to get a "good night's sleep." Go to bed with the knowingness that you have done all you can do for the day, and now it's time to restore and repair your body and mind. If you need to make a to-do list before you retire for the night, by all means do it if it will help to clear your mind. You may also want to check your local health food store for homeopathic sleep remedies that are non-habit forming and non-addictive.

Relationships - When you're caring for a family member, it's easy to dissolve your life into that person's and mistakenly assume that the other important people in your life will understand. They may initially understand that you are going through a tough time, but as time passes and you withdraw more energy from your spouse or partner, children, and other friends and family members, they may feel neglected and hurt. Do your best to nurture these relationships and reach out to those you care about and who care about you. Express yourself and try to be open about what you are going through; this will give others a chance to be empathetic towards you and perhaps offer to assist you in caring for your loved one.

Hobbies/Fun - Whatever you do, don't give up doing what you enjoy, it can be a lifesaver. You may need to be flexible with how often, but make it a priority to schedule and continue to participate in the activities that give you pleasure. If you are having to spend time "sitting" with a loved one you may want to take part in a creative project, such as scrapbooking, painting, or reading and learning about a new topic that has been of interest to you. Utilizing some kind of creative outlet is therapeutic and relaxing and certainly not a waste of time. Make sure you see friends and laugh often. If you are having a difficult time laughing or finding anything about life funny, watch a hilarious TV program or a movie that you already know makes you laugh.

Journaling – Expressing your thoughts, feelings, and experiences by writing them in a journal is a powerful tool for mental and emotional health. A journal can become a best friend of sorts; always there to listen, never judge, and help you to gain valuable insight about what you're truly feeling. Even if you only write a few sentences at the end of the day, journaling can help transform difficult emotions and confusion into an epiphany.

Reading – I am the kind of person (not everyone is) that finds value in reading about what challenge I may be facing. When I knew my dad was going to die from cancer, I read books about facing the death of a loved one, about losing parents, and philosophical books about life and death that helped me to gain insight, wisdom, and the strength I needed to face the situation. Locate your own comfort zone, but I highly recommend books that restore faith and offer hope for healing and wellness. No matter where we find ourselves in life, someone else has been there before us and can offer us inspiration and valuable tools for coping with our circumstances.

Exercise - Even though it may seem as if you don't possibly have enough time to exercise, it is highly recommended that you do take the time, even if it is a short walk each day. Exercise increases circulation and releases brain chemicals that assist in elevating our moods. When my mom was living with me and on hospice, I was stretched in ways emotionally I never thought possible. My saving grace was my early morning run by the sea. I would write her a note, place it at her bedside, and quietly exit to make this happen. I still remember how grateful I was to smell the salt air, feel the breeze, and move along the shore. It felt as if I was shaking all the stress off and centering myself to begin the day. During that time, I was also lucky enough to see many dolphins close to shore. It was if they knew to greet me each morning, and at times, the sight of them brought tears to my eyes. I stayed about ten minutes past my run to breathe, meditate, and say a sincere prayer of intention for the day. I continued this routine until about two weeks before my mom died. With further decline, I felt I needed to be at her side, but when someone could sit with her in my place,

I did fit in my running, which was so helpful in keeping me strong and sane during this most difficult time. Very often, my journaling material came from the contemplation I did during my runs. If you don't already have some exercise routine that works for you, please find one. Whether it's the gym, yoga or a Pilates class, a walk, a bike ride, or a nice run, do it and don't feel guilty for the time it takes. It will make you a better and more present (Zen like) caregiver. When we love ourselves well, we love others better, too.

Nutrition - It can be a challenge to make sound decisions about nutrition, but it is essential to eat and drink well, especially when we are demanding so much of ourselves physically and emotionally. Do the best you can to eat fresh fruits and vegetables, lean meats and fish, and stay away from high sodium, high sugar, and high fat, fried and packaged foods. In addition, try to avoid consuming aspartame and other artificial sweeteners, as there are numerous serious physical and psychological side effects that simply make ingesting them not worth the risk. It may seem faster and easier to grab these types of food on the run, but there are consequences, and one of the consequences is that we don't feel as well after ingesting these types of foods. When you begin to establish new habits of eating healthy, you will also begin to correlate a clear mind, strong energy, calmness and "lightness" to these new eating habits. Be sure to drink plenty of pure water as well. Most sources say eight 8 ounce glasses per day, but for years now most nutritionists have agreed that the right amount is half your weight in ounces per day. For example, if you weigh one hundred and forty pounds, you should drink seventy ounces of water per day. Do your best to limit caffeine and alcohol. You may want to experiment with herbal teas that suit your taste and purpose. For example, chamomile tea is wonderful for relaxation and/or as a sleeping aid.

While it may be difficult to create the time to utilize some of these modalities, I want to underscore how potentially helpful the one that is "right for you" and/or your parent can be. Many of these methods can soften the sharp edges of your experience and truly help to improve the quality of yours and your parent's lives and the journey you are taking together.

"Before you uproot your parent from his or her home, please explore every option and do everything possible to include them in the decision."

Cheryl A. Kuba

CHAPTER EIGHT
When Is It Time For Placement?

Knowing when it is time to suggest and help your parent(s) move from their home can be a very difficult decision. Making a major move is obviously much easier when a person is healthy, but as we have discussed, most people's original plan is to age in place in perfect control of the day's schedule and atmosphere. Many people are attached to the home that they first purchased when they were young adults, raised their children and thus far, enjoyed the peace and quiet of retirement in the environment where they feel most familiar. I was lucky that my parent's hobby was to donate furniture, buy new, and move from new environment to new environment. Perhaps this took the place of world travel, but they called each move an adventure and truly appeared to enjoy the process of looking for a new place and then getting it set-up the way they liked. They had no resistance to the idea of downsizing and simplifying their lives by renting an "independent senior apartment." This is not the case with many older adults needing to make a change.

Letting go of what they have known for so long can be terribly painful. Many people are attached to the gardens they have nurtured for years or the workshop and tools in the garage. When it does come time for a necessary move , do your very best to be sensitive and understanding in the process. Remember, many people fear losing control of their lives, as well as their independence. A move from the family home may feel like the beginning of this dreaded occurrence. Before this decision is made, you may want to check in your area for facilities that provide respite stays: temporary stays to offer families a break from providing care. You may also want to consider hiring a live-in caregiver for long weekends so you can have a break from your caregiving duties.

Make sure the facility is interested in knowing who your parent is and what's important to them. Get to know the rules of where your parent is, what they will be providing, and how you can still participate in their lives. Many caregivers still want to provide care, on some level, for their parent even after they go to live in some type of facility. It is natural to experience grief and relief simultaneously after someone is placed. If you were forced to make the decision because your parent was not capable, you may feel guilty and question whether or not it was the right decision. Be prepared for an adjustment period for you and your parent after a move is made to a facility.

Some older adults, such as my own parents, look forward to relinquishing the responsibilities that go along with owning and maintaining a home. Seniors who have had neighbors, friends, spouses, and partners die may also feel lonely and isolated so moving to congregate living may feel appealing to them. Regardless of how you or your parent(s) feel about this decision, it would probably be extremely helpful for you to visit several places of "senior living" for it may be much different than what any of you are imagining. I think we all have said to ourselves, or heard another say, "Don't put me in a nursing home, I'd rather die if I can't take care of myself." It's important to know that there are many "in-between" choices to make when it comes to senior living.

HOW DO YOU KNOW IT'S TIME?

The following points are some important criteria to consider when deciding to place someone in a facility.

- Is the physical care beyond the primary family caregiver's ability?

- Is pain management too difficult to control?
- Is the older adult no longer able to recognize the primary family caregiver?
- Is the financial means of paying for in-home professional caregivers almost depleted?
- Is the physical and emotional strain of the older adult's care jeopardizing the health and well-being of the primary family caregiver?

SAFETY

Sometimes, even after modifying the home and putting a professional caregiver in place, safety and wellness remain an issue. For example, when one spouse has dementia that causes wandering, agitation, incontinence, and they no longer recognize their loved ones. Paying for homecare 24/7 may become cost prohibitive at a certain point. This type of care is different from having a live-in caregiver who can sleep at night. Hourly care, which provides around-the-clock supervision, is extremely expensive.

WHAT KIND OF ENVIRONMENT IS BEST FOR MY PARENT?

Of course, the type of senior living arrangement you choose depends upon the health and well-being of your parents. If they are cognitively able, the decision is theirs to make and perhaps they will appreciate your assistance in researching the various options in living environments. It is so important to educate yourself about the various options in "senior living," as well as what your parent or family can afford.

LIVING OPTIONS

I realize it would be very helpful for me to offer more information about costs in this section; however, expenses can vary widely depending upon where you live and what a person will need. Consult a local area placement specialist, Area Agency on Aging, or community centers for ranges of cost where your parent will be living.

INDEPENDENT/ACTIVE SENIOR APARTMENTS

Independent Senior Housing refers to housing that is restricted to adults, usually age 50 and older, although some buildings may include younger adults with disabilities. These facilities represent a tenant-landlord relationship where the owner/operator has no responsibility to supervise or provide personal care. This type of housing generally does not include supportive services to address the special needs of aging residents. Independent apartments are not licensed or monitored by government housing agencies. Each apartment is set-up with lower cabinets, wider doorways, grab bars in bathrooms, and showers that allow for safe entry and exit. Most senior apartment complexes have a common area for socializing, reading, watching television, and playing games. Some will offer limited transportation; for example, a van that takes residents to the grocery store each Tuesday. The cost will vary, just as it does for any type of apartment complex. Some senior apartments are HUD-subsidized (U.S. Department of Housing and Urban Development) for individuals with low incomes.

SENIOR COMMUNITY (PLANNED RETIREMENT COMMUNITY)

Independent living for seniors, sometimes called "Active 55+ Communities." Generally, in this environment people purchase their home or condo. Some communities do not allow people to carry a mortgage on the property. They usually offer amenities such as organized social programs, clubs, classes, and transportation. Some have golf courses, tennis courts, bowling, churches, and other amenities. Cost will vary widely depending upon the amenities, the location, and size of the condominium or home.

CONTINUUM OF CARE RETIREMENT COMMUNITY (CCRC)

A large planned community in a campus-like setting that offers all levels of care: independent living, assisted living, and skilled nursing. Some have specialized Alzheimer's units. There is normally a large "buy-in" amount and the resident receives assistance and the necessary level of care for the remainder of their lives. Be sure to thoroughly read the contract for important details about requirements and refund percentages if your parent passes away shortly after moving in.

MEMORY CARE

If your parent has some form of dementia beyond the early stages, you'll want to find out if the assisted-living facility separates residents with dementia. Many have a special "wing" devoted to memory care. They are decorated beautifully in many facilities and the fact that they're secured areas is very subtle. You will want to observe some important things about the facility.

- Is it calm and quiet?
- Do they play music?
- Is it well lit?
- Are there complex patterns on the walls or carpets? This can be disruptive for a person with dementia.
- Is the staff able to see and observe common areas and rooms?
- Does the facility have picture cues for functioning? For example, a picture of a toilet on the bathroom door.
- Do they have a wander alert system?
- Is there a secured area for walking?
- Do you agree with the facility's philosophy of care?
- As your parent's disease progresses, will they be able to remain at this facility?
- What is the facility's philosophy on using physical restraints for certain behaviors?
- What type of activities do they provide?
- Do they do periodic night checks?
- How many staff are there and awake during the night?
- What type of training is required for the staff?
- Does the facility have a support group?
- Are there additional charges for increased needs?

ASSISTED LIVING (ALF)

Assisted living is an option for people who want to remain as independent as possible, but their ability to do so has become limited. An ALF is licensed to accommodate residents in a protected environment with additional supervision for hygiene, medication, diet, and ambulation. Do your homework and ensure that the "culture" of the facility is a match for your parent. Make sure this facility, or any other, is sincerely interested in learning about what is important to your parent(s).

An entity that uses the term "assisted living" must be licensed and regulated by the state and must provide or arrange for the following:

- On-site monitoring 24/7
- Daily food service
- Personal care services and home care services, including help with grooming, dressing, bathing, and eating (either directly or indirectly)
- Case management
- Housekeeping/laundry
- Activities and recreational opportunities
- Medication assistance and medication supervision

The environment in assisted-living facilities varies widely. Some have separate areas for residents with memory impairment and others do not. Many have the feel of home and offer various activities throughout the day. Some have resident birds, cats, and dogs. Some will bring in a pianist a few times a week to play for the residents. When people move into an ALF there is very often a dramatic adjustment period. Think of it as going to a new school when you were young and you're the "new kid on the block." It is no different in this situation. Residents have their "cliques" and can be resistant to letting outsiders in. They eat lunch together, play bingo together, walk together, and "reserve" the couch together for movie night. It may take a while, but most people do adjust and make new friends. An ALF can be quite expensive - $3,000-$6,000 a month or more.

RESIDENTIAL CARE FACILITY (RCFE)

These facilities provide room and board, supervision, and personal-care assistance. In California, there are small six-bed facilities operating out of regular homes and licensed by the state to provide care. You'll want to do your homework ahead of time to ensure the facility is safe, nurturing, and a fit for your parent. Culture, food, location, quality of staff, and environment are all important things to consider. In addition, affordability, activities, and services provided are all important things to consider. For example, do they take residents with dementia or do they have a hospice waiver in case your parent goes on hospice while in their care? Make an appointment with the facility administrator and ask questions. In addition, visit unannounced to get a true feel for the environment. If you are not welcome to show up without an appointment, this facility may not be a good choice for your parent. Typically, RCFEs are more affordable than a large assisted-living facility, but costs vary depending upon location and services needed. Every state does not offer this option. Check with your parent's local Area Agency on Aging.

SKILLED NURSING FACILITY (SNF)

Facilities for patients who need twenty-four-hour nursing supervision, many of whom are confined to bed for all or some portion of the day. Many SNFs are not the bleak, isolating facilities of the past. The walls have color and pictures; many offer activities, music therapy, and art for those that are able to participate. Dementia and incontinence are the primary two reasons a person is admitted to a SNF. Usually the level of care needed has become unmanageable for family members. Due to the high number of staff required to provide twenty-four-hour care, the cost for a SNF is high, about $70,000 per year (Hogan, 2010). Medicare only pays for short term care when the patient is relatively capable of rehabilitation. After a person's assets are exhausted, it will be necessary to apply for Medicaid to pay the facility for the care of your parent. Not every nursing home accepts Medicaid reimbursement. If you think your parent's finances will be exhausted, make sure the SNF where you are admitting your parent is a participant in the state-run welfare program.

Medical Model Versus Social Model - A culture change in long-term care facilities involves a shift in philosophy and practice from an overemphasis on safety, uniformity, and medical issues toward resident-directed, consumer-driven health promotion and quality of life. Fundamental to this shift is a focus on the importance of the relationships between residents and direct-care staff. For example, the Eden Alternative is an international not-for-profit organization dedicated to transforming care environments into habitats for human beings that promote quality of life for all involved. It is a powerful tool for inspiring well-being for older adults and those who collaborate with them as care partners. The Eden Alternative's principle-based philosophy empowers care partners to transform institutional approaches of care into the creation of a community where life is worth living. If I seem biased, you're right. I think that whenever it's possible to include care that focuses on the overall well-being of a person, that choice is the best one. In addition, the well-being of the staff is considered in these environments; in my opinion, everybody wins. Eden offers education to a variety of care partners and its philosophy can be integrated into the home, as well as in long-term care settings. (www.edenalt.org).

USING A PLACEMENT SPECIALIST

If you are confused about the needs and desires of your parent(s) or what they can afford, it may be extremely helpful to use the services of a qualified placement specialist. This professional will sit down with your family and gather all of this information from you and your parents. They will then take you to see various options that may be appropriate for your parent(s). You do not pay for this service, but if your family chooses one of the facilities your specialist has shown you, the facility pays them a referral fee. Using a placement specialist can save you a tremendous amount of time you may spend doing research and then visiting the different options.

ELDERLAW SPECIALIST

If your parent's financial resources are limited, contact an Elderlaw specialist to discuss planning and to determine if your parent is eligible for any type of assistance. If you need guidance finding the help you need, contact your parent's local Area Agency on Aging.

THE EMOTIONS OF PLACEMENT

Some people gain a sense of peace once their parent has been moved to some type of senior living environment. They feel their parent is now safe and being looked after on a regular basis, and they can now turn their focus back to their own lives. Other adult children question the decision made, by either their parent or themselves, to move them into a senior-living situation. They experience guilt and perceive the move as a failure on their part. Others feel they have broken a promise made long ago; for example, "Promise me you'll never put me in a nursing home?" The reply, "I promise Mom, I would never do such a thing to you." Many caregivers want to still provide some level of care for their parent, even after they are placed. Become familiar with the facility's rules and schedules so you are not perceived as a hindrance, but as a cooperative and caring family member and care partner. Remember, you are still a caregiver and advocate for your parent.

Expect that you may have some type of reaction to your parent's change in living arrangement, especially if it is a sudden necessity. For example, if you and your family have been gathering for many years for the holidays in the home where you grew up, it may be painful and emotionally upsetting to suddenly have to make other plans. Eventually, we build new traditions and may even come to realize that we are enjoying these new traditions and had actually felt trapped and obligated by what we had been doing for so many years. You may find it helpful to take advantage of some of the tools explained in Chapter Seven to assist you through this situation.

Do your best to avoid making a decision for placement in a crisis. If you are rushed and have to find a place with "an opening" or an available bed, you are not likely to have the time to consider important factors in maintaining a quality of life for your parent. Do your homework now by learning what is important to your parent – don't make assumptions – have the conversations and listen. Make sure the facility cares about your parent as an individual, and is not just trying to fill their beds with warm bodies. Everything is important. The food, the music, the language spoken, the décor, and the indoor and outdoor surroundings are all important things to consider. Remember, the goal is for your parent to feel at home, as much as possible, whatever that means to them. Bring some of their furniture to the facility and hang their favorite pictures on the walls. You may want to have their family photo album there so the staff can get to know them through these cherished photographs. Create a profile of your parent so that the staff understands your parent's life and that it had, and continues to have, meaning. Include in the profile where they were born, where their parents were born, how many siblings they have, where they grew up, their occupation, their hobbies and talents. In addition, include their daily routine and preferences.

AN OMBUDSMAN IS YOUR RESOURCE

An Ombudsman is a trained advocate who empowers residents in long-term care facilities and their families. They are educated in the rights, needs, and issues of residents. In addition, they are educated about the local and state regulations that govern long-term care facilities. The Long-Term Care Ombudsman is a federally and state mandated program that investigates any suspected abuse or neglect. They make unannounced visits to the facilities to accurately see how the facility operates. They also speak to residents who perceive a problem or simply sit and listen to their complaints. The intention of the Ombudsman is to help residents and families become effective advocates and to improve the quality of life for residents in these facilities. All licensed, skilled nursing and residential care facilities are required by law to display an Ombudsman poster listing the services they provide and a contact number. If you have concerns about your parent's care, don't hesitate to contact your Ombudsman, it is confidential (Council on Aging, Orange County, 2012).

"Death ends a life, not a relationship."

MITCH ALBOM

CHAPTER NINE
Fear And Love

*O*ne of the most cherished days I spent with my dad was also one of the most heart wrenching. He had been receiving immune therapy intravenously. Even so, he was growing weaker, the tumor in his lung was growing, and he was becoming tired of the rigorous routine he was enduring to please his family and to hopefully prolong the inevitability of his approaching death. We both knew it. The weight of grief and sadness sat on my shoulders like a herd of elephants. As always, I was sitting with him while he received his treatment in a room full of people who sat in recliners configured in a semi-circle so they could to take in the beautiful view outside. In silence, with no words spoken, we both were acknowledging our sadness, our feelings of defeat and dreaded separation. I held my dad's warm hand and memorized all of its characteristics: the color, the perfectly manicured fingernails, each vein, the lines on the palm, the size, and how it pulsated with such profound love. Yes, even though in that moment I felt heartbroken and isolated in my pain because no other human being could share the enormity of the private and personal loss I was feeling; simultaneously I was experiencing what I would describe as my heart being a wide open space filled with more love than could possibly be contained. It was moving through all of me and all around me. The trivialities of life, even the grief of losing my dad, had been suspended in time and all that remained was pure love. This moment was a profound realization for me to know that we don't have to choose or decide if we are feeling good or bad. We don't have to categorize our emotions and stick with them, but instead we can allow them to ebb and flow, and the agony and joy of a moment can co-exist with even the most neutral of feelings.

I discovered, in those few moments, an incredible sense of empowerment because I experienced the two extremes of emotions at the same time, helping me know that I could face my most dreaded fears and pass through them because it's all temporary. When we avoid these difficult emotions by resisting them, trying to go around them, under them, over them, or by denying their presence, we exhaust ourselves and become more uncomfortable and disconnected from the truth. For my dad and me there was a sense of relief between us because we had gently embraced the truth. We could now relax and be real with the time that remained.

Breaking through and acknowledging the fear of loss can be very painful, but so can the avoidance of what is really going on. Avoidance is easily recognized when we find ourselves, in the midst of a terminal diagnosis, talking about the weather or commenting critically about the outfit the newscaster is wearing. We may become irritable and angry as we try to keep what we are really feeling under cover. Acknowledging the truth and being sincere with one another usually frees us up to experience more rewarding experiences.

"Realization of the immortal self is not always easy, even with the urgency of our physical decline."
J. Phillip Jones

END OF LIFE

END OF LIFE WISHES

Hopefully, your parent(s) had their documents completed, and you are well aware of their wishes for healthcare and end-of-life issues, as well as burial, cremation, and other spiritual and ceremonial desires. It is important for you to truly understand their wishes for life-sustaining care and under what circumstances, before you are faced with making such a decision. Many people have definite feelings about being buried or not being buried, cremated or not being cremated. Just think for a moment about how you feel about these issues. It is advised that all of us preplan our funerals so our families don't have to do so under duress. We are less likely to spend more than necessary when the death has not yet occurred. It is becoming more and more common for individuals to share in advance just how they would like to be honored after they die. It is so much easier to talk about these things when we are healthy, rather than when death is staring us in the face; however, even if death is imminent, ask questions and try to find out what is important to your parent.

PALLIATIVE CARE AND HOSPICE

Palliative care focuses on keeping a person comfortable rather than focusing on the illness(s) the person is experiencing. This type of care gives the person control over treatment and considers and honors the person's goals and priorities. Palliative care is for people who are chronically ill, perhaps with heart disease and arthritis, but are not dying. Perhaps the person has been in and out of the hospital on a regular basis so they choose to be treated at home in the future and avoid hospital stays. Hospice, on the other hand, is for people who are at the end stage of an illness. Hospice supports the patient and the family and often extends the life of the patient rather than ending it, as some people believe. Yes, it's true that very often the empathetic care, which includes: pain and symptom relief, psychosocial care, spiritual counseling, and an end to running from doctor to doctor, helps a person feel better, and they may live longer than they might have otherwise. The intent of hospice is to provide medical care that focuses on making the time that a person has left to be quality time. It is a myth that hospice is about overmedicating a person to the point of causing their death. I believe this myth to be common because so many families and/or doctors wait until death is nearly imminent before they will sign a person onto hospice care that they die a few days or even hours after service begins. When I was an intern and eventual volunteer for hospice, one patient I visited was under the care of hospice for nearly two years.

It is my belief and observation that when an interest is shown in how we feel emotionally, and we are asked about our life and what's important to us, we take an interest in ourselves and often this re-engages in our own life. This can be a profound time of reflection, healing, and exploring what our life has meant, and what our impact on others has been. At its best, it is a time of deep forgiveness, not only for others, but self-forgiveness as well. Consider that this may happen for your parent. Do your best to be present and aware so you don't miss the opportunity of witnessing this cherished gift.

"It often said that it is not death that we fear, but the dying process itself; the pain, the shortness of breath, and the thought of being alone when we die." Unknown

---

Conversations about the dying process can be very difficult and uncomfortable. Hospice professionals can help guide a family through the journey. It is so valuable to ask a person what they most fear or what concerns them the most. For example, "I am so worried that my wife will not be taken care of." Or, "I am so afraid no one will take my dog in and care for her." Often, people are afraid they are going to go to hell and having a Rabbi, Reverend, Pastor, or other spiritual advisor or mentor to speak with, pray with or meditate with, can help to resolve these fears. We all wish to die in peace, whatever that definition of peace is for us. What more important gift is there to offer in life than doing your best to honor a person and help them transition from this world with a quiet, resolved mind, and an open, peaceful heart?

HOSPICE FACTS

- No one is forced onto hospice–a consent form must be signed, either by the person or the person designated to make healthcare decisions on the advanced healthcare directive. For example, "If my death from a terminal condition is imminent and even if life-sustaining procedures were to be used, there is no reasonable expectation of my recovery, I direct my life not be extended by life-sustaining procedures." In such a case, the person may specify they want painkillers, but not a feeding tube (Hogan, 2010).
- The decision to go on hospice care is revocable. A person may be on hospice for a time, but then decide to take part in an experimental treatment (Hogan, 2010).
- The primary focus of hospice is comfort and pain control.
- Hospice is covered by Medicare.
- Most health insurance plans cover hospice.
- Most often, 90 percent of hospice care is delivered in the home; however, it can be provided in the hospital or nursing home. There are also some "hospice houses," dedicated to hospice care.
- The typical hospice team includes: a physician, a nurse, home-health aide, social worker, and a chaplain for any religious or spiritual practice. The team also includes volunteers to provide visits and respite for family.

Hospice care supports the entire family, not just the patient. I can remember one long night when my dad was having so much trouble breathing. I called hospice around 1:00 a.m. to discuss what I should do. It meant so much to me to be able to talk to another person at that hour that was qualified to offer me helpful suggestions and guidance in the middle of the night. They are there to keep your loved one safe and comfortable and also there to alleviate your fears and concerns as you navigate what is, for most people, unchartered, and often frightening territory.

RELIGION AND SPIRITUALITY

Western culture, for the most part, avoids thinking about death or acknowledging its inevitability. Many people choose to believe "IT" won't happen to them. We say things like, "If I die," instead of "When I die." Even then, many of us envision ourselves climbing into bed at ninety-nine-years-old and quietly going to sleep and drifting off to heaven. I have had the honor of being at the bedsides of several people whose deaths were drawing near. Once, I sat by the side of an eighty-seven-year-old woman who was dying in a beautiful assisted living facility, unfortunately she had no family or friends. She kept a bible at her bedside and often spoke of church experiences. She expressed to me repeatedly of her fear of going to hell. I asked her why she even imagined that she would be going to hell. The worst behavior she could come up with was that of stealing a grape (probably unknowingly) as a young child. Her mother most likely used the occasion to put the fear of God into her daughter by informing her that children who steal will burn in hell. Using fear to get people to conform and follow rules is common in Western culture, but in my opinion, offers little more than blind faith as death approaches.

When my mom was recovering in a nursing home, I pointed to a beautiful painting of Jesus that her roommate had on the wall and asked my mom if that brought her comfort. She quickly replied, "No, I don't want him coming for me." When people become aware that that they are dying, they often ponder the meaning of their life and ask questions, such as: "Who am I?" "Who is God?" "Have I been a good person?" "How will I be judged in the afterlife?" You may want to ask your parent if they'd like to talk to a member of the clergy so they may, hopefully, resolve their fears and take comfort in their religion or spiritual beliefs.

Cultures and spiritual practices of the East teach us to ask philosophical questions as a part of a life-long journey of searching, understanding, and realizing a deep knowingness of who we are beyond the physical body. Buddhism teaches us that by acknowledging our own immortality, we are better able to live full and enriching lives. Buddhists practice their own death by meditating on it, envisioning it, and facing the fear of it. Eastern religions view the physical body as a beautiful gift, but focus on remembering that the body is not their true identity. Meditation is strongly encouraged in order to have ongoing spiritual experiences beyond the body, to prevent the attachment that so often leads to suffering. I'm not suggesting that if you are a Christian you become a Buddhist, but I think contemplating these deeper thoughts of who you are as a spiritual being can be helpful in facing your own mortality and that of your parents.

If we live our lives in a way that denies that we will one day die, and we are then informed that we have an incurable disease, we are forced into our own intense grief, as a result. For those who take life for granted, assuming they have all the time in the world to experience what they desire, the grief can be overwhelming. My dad sobbed when I helped him clean out his office and pack things so my parents could move closer to me. As we hugged he said, "I kept thinking I would have time to do something with all of this and now my life is over." The gift of the moment was him unknowingly suggesting to me that I don't make the same mistake by taking time for granted.

I teach a caregiver workshop that touches on the topic of hospice. Just as soon as the slide appears on the screen the energy drops in the room to one of sadness. Many people view the role of hospice as a giving-up on their loved one. Many families even request that their dying loved one not be told they are on hospice. Or, as in my family, it took us a very long time to be completely honest with my mom about my dad's terminal diagnosis. Sadly, she was aware of what was happening, and we didn't allow her the space to discuss her fears and concerns until we were deep into the journey.

END OF LIFE GIFTS

When my mom was in the hospital, with her COPD, destabilized upon her contemplation of life without my dad, I had the opportunity to spend some healing time with my dad. Up until that time, my dad never brought up the past and how his alcoholism impacted me as a child. I think him seeing me spring into action to help during the time of crisis reminded him of me tirelessly trying to help him when I was a child and adolescent. He spoke of the time I took him to the doctor when I was nineteen because his drinking had nearly destroyed his physical body, and he couldn't function. He was so ill and shaking so badly he couldn't hold a glass of water. I can still recall the sadness, worry, and exhaustion I felt as I reassured him all would be okay if he would just stop drinking. When the doctor completed the exam he told me to take him directly to the hospital. Later, after running tests, he told my dad if he took another drink, he'd be dead in thirty days. This is what it took for him to become sober. Soon after, I moved out of my parent's home. With my mom and dad sober, I felt I could finally begin to have my own life. We called a silent truce to the years of chaos and never spoke of it again.

There we were, twenty years later at an acupuncturist appointment, and I was helping him put on his shoes, and he said through tears, "You were there for me then and you're here for me now." This opened up a conversation that was incredibly validating and healing for me. My dad felt so ashamed and guilty that he had caused his lung cancer through years of smoking; another self-destructive addiction had ravaged his body. He was so angry that this time he wouldn't be able to cheat it and come out alive. His revelations broke my heart, but at the same time, his acknowledgement that I had feelings and was deeply affected, then and now, meant the world to me. In that moment, I was finally real and no longer just a machine of strength and duty, expected to fix everything. Nearly twenty years later I received an apology I never expected and never dreamed possible. I remain so grateful and appreciative.

A year-and-half later my mom was on hospice and living with me. It was the evening before what would be her last Thanksgiving. She was weak, thin, and constantly troubled by shortness of breath. I had helped her take a shower and was drying her legs when she began to cry. She so sweetly expressed, "I'm not crying because I'm sad, I'm crying because I'm so filled with love for you." Even now, nearly ten years later, I often hear her statement in my mind, and it means the world to me. My mom and I had some very difficult times through the years. We had a relationship that, even with the presence of many wonderful moments, contained animosity, turmoil, and disappointment for both of us. When she shared her touching remark so spontaneously, I knew her love for me was real.

These are just two examples of the many gifts I received when my parents were at the end of their lives. Moments like these are what make the difficulty of the journey so rewarding, so fulfilling. Do your best to spend time with your parent that is quiet and unhurried so you have a better chance of capturing these kinds of tender experiences. When you're stressed for lack of time and racing in and out to simply check on your parent or complete tasks unconsciously, moments like these are unlikely.

ACCEPTING THE DYING PROCESS

Eventually, a person at the end stage of life will stop leaving their home; even for short activities, such as going out to lunch. They will initially spend time in the living room and socialize, taking naps when they need to. As time passes, they will remain in bed and begin to lose interest in once enjoyed television shows or reading the newspaper. They will begin to lose their ability to talk on the telephone. You will notice they are sleeping more and more.

"Death is not an anomaly or the most dreaded of all events as modern culture would have you believe, but the most natural thing in the world, inseparable from and just as natural as its polarity---birth. Remind yourself of this when you sit with a dying person." Eckhart Tolle

---

"Allowing" someone to die may seem counter intuitive. When your parent stops eating and drinking it can be very distressing. It is a major sign that they are detaching from this world. As best you can, try to accept this as a natural part of the life cycle and not something you can control. Forcing them to eat or drink will not help at a certain point, and, in fact, may be harmful.

Our human bodies, once they are finished struggling to live, know what to do in order to die. When a person is close to death, they naturally lose their appetite and only want drops of water on their lips and mouth for moisture. The organs are shutting down and the body no longer needs food and water; there is no desire. Forcing food and liquids into someone who can no longer digest, circulate, or dispose of them can cause complications; such as, shortness of breath, fluid in the lungs, sever constipation, diarrhea, bloating and infections, making the person more uncomfortable (Morris 2004).

TERMINAL RESTLESSNESS OR AGITATION

Many families may be surprised when a terminally ill (and usually calm) family member becomes restless or even agitated. The depth of such restlessness or agitation varies from person to person. My mom and dad both had pretty severe terminal agitation. Moods change or personalities seem to change, family members may be completely bewildered and feel helpless, not knowing what to do. When a terminal illness not only initially strikes, but is now nearing the end, patients may experience profound mood changes. Such mood changes are often difficult for family members to "handle." Causes and treatments for restlessness and agitation are well known among the palliative care professionals who work with the dying on a regular basis. If you have this experience with your parent, the hospice team will be a helpful support in explaining to you what is occurring and why. They will also help your mother or father with the appropriate medications to alleviate their discomfort and distress (www.hospicepatients.org).

It is natural to wonder what to expect as your loved one prepares to die, but perhaps you are afraid to ask. If your parent is indeed on hospice, you will be given reading material which explains the signs of imminent death. In addition, the hospice nurse will answer your questions and guide you through this process. The way a person dies varies from person to person. Some people take longer, some pass away gently in their sleep before the family is expecting it, some slip into a coma, and still others remain somewhat alert until they die. It may be difficult to read about the signs of approaching death, but if you know in advance what may occur you will be better prepared and less frightened when you observe it. Not every person experiences every sign of approaching death, but it usually looks similar.

SOME SIGNS YOU MAY OBSERVE

- Your parent may become thinner from not eating.
- They may have difficulty breathing, nausea, vomiting, constipation, diarrhea, or confusion.
- They become stiff from lying in bed.
- They may sleep a lot and irregularly.
- They may not talk very much.
- They may carry on conversations with others who have already passed away.
- They may think they're in another place; such as, a home they lived in many years ago.
- As death approaches their extremities may feel cold and look discolored.
- They may have a spike in body temperature.
- They may experience the "the death rattle," a sound caused by the throat muscles relaxing and secretions gathering, making a gurgling sound. This sound may be distressing to you, but it doesn't mean your parent is uncomfortable.
- There may be gaps in breathing for a few seconds. The gaps will become longer as death approaches.

- Sometimes, as the body fully relaxes, the bowels and bladder release upon death.
- Sometimes a person's eyes and/or jaw remain open after they die.
- Some will yell or make an attempt to stand. Try to remember that while this may be upsetting to you and your family, the person is not suffering. The effort is largely reflexive and not a conscious one.

(Morris, 2004)

Once my dad's agitation was taken care of, he became very peaceful. His last few days were spent telling us over and over again that he loved us. As he slipped into a coma for the last time, he did so with love on his lips. "I love you," were his last words. My mom struggled and fought the process. Her last words were not as peaceful as my dad's. At the time, it was extremely difficult for me to accept that my mom died seemingly angry with me. In my own mind, I had done everything humanly possible to "make" her comfortable, safe, and unafraid. My lifetime of efforts spent trying to bring her happiness seemed to have failed. It all felt like a cruel joke. I sat on my stairs, dumbfounded and devastated, as the mortuary attendants respectfully wheeled my mom's body out my front door for the last time. It was over, and my mom and I would now never be "okay." At the time, I couldn't know that the seemingly horrible "end" would later be a catharsis for profound healing.

AFTER DEATH

After your parent dies, you have a right to be with their body to continue saying good-bye, hold them, pray, or just be present. You may wait for others to arrive to say good-bye. You may want to bathe them or groom them in some way and dress them. Some people feel this is a way to honor a loved one. My mom, brother, and I dressed my dad in his favorite pajamas. We simply didn't feel right about allowing him to "go out" in a t-shirt and a diaper.

If your parent is on hospice, the mortuary you are using will already be known. You will call hospice to notify them of your parent's death. They will send a nurse to make the declaration that your parent has indeed died. They will then call the mortuary to come and take the body to the mortuary. If your parent dies in the hospital, you will call the nurse when you are ready, and the nurse will take it from there. You are welcome to ask for a member of the clergy to be called. The funeral home will begin the process of completing the death certificate and preparing the body for the cremation or burial. If you were not physically present for your parent's death and wanted to be, know that there are many accounts of people "waiting" until they were alone to die. Do your best not to feel guilty. It's also perfectly acceptable for you to ask others who may have been present what occurred during your parent's last hours and moment of death (Morris, 2004).

If your parent's funeral has not been pre-planned and you need to find a funeral director, ask friends and family members for a referral in the area so you work with someone reputable. It is recommended that you use a locally owned and operated funeral home so you receive more personal service. If you are planning the funeral from a distance, ask your reputable local funeral director for a referral. If you don't already have a member of the clergy whom you'd like to officiate, the funeral home can give you a referral (Morris, 2004). You may also want to consider doing something like a dove or balloon release to honor your parent. These unique rituals are often what is clearly remembered from a service and may bring you comfort as time passes.

THE IMPORTANCE OF A FUNERAL OR CEREMONY

"REMEMBER ME LIKE THIS"

"How do you want to be remembered?" I know of one woman who wants her funeral to be decorated in the theme of Christmas, regardless of the time of year. I also recently heard of a gentleman who passed away in his early fifties. Each year he and his wife and children would visit the zoo on Father's Day. The family had his "Celebration of Life" service at the zoo. Apparently, the zoo had already been beautifully decorated for a holiday event. A family member shared with me the sacredness of the wolves lying down in a line to watch the ceremony. In another moment, a flock of geese flew over the group at a serendipitous time.

Ceremony is important and is the beginning of the healing process for those who are left behind to gather the pieces and move forward with their own lives.

At both my mom and dad's services, we released doves. In addition to the doves, we had a gentleman play the bagpipes at my dad's service. Even with my dad's openness about many things, he was never able to express how he wanted to be remembered or what he wanted in terms of a service. My mom expressed certain things as her death became more imminent. Ideally, what a person wants is expressed well in advance of their death: burial, cremation, burial at sea, a green funeral, or ashes scattered or buried and where exactly? My mom specifically stated that she wanted to be buried in a blue dress. My brother and I went shopping the day after she died and reached in through opposite sides of the dress rack only to put our hands on the same blue dress, it was as if our mom was there choosing it herself.

I know many people who have already chosen what music will be played at their "celebration of life." One dear friend of mine died sooner than expected during the holiday season. The only local place that had an open time for a service that worked for family and friends was a beautiful equestrian center with open time on a cold, December evening. It was beautifully decorated with Christmas lights and other signs of holiday festivities. It turned out to be the perfect place to honor, remember, and celebrate our dear friend with music, a slide show, photographs, and numerous eulogies that tenderly expressed how she had impacted so many of us.

If your parent simply won't talk about what they desire or circumstances are such that you can't gather the information, it is highly recommended that you still have some type of service. Reach out to friends for a referral to a trusted funeral director or other person who can guide you and educate you about all of the different options. A ceremony does not need to cost a lot of money; it can be friends and family gathering on a beach or in the mountains and sharing stories about the one who has passed away. The support of other family members, friends of your parents, your friends, or perhaps your parent's neighbors, gathering together and honoring your mom or dad in ceremony can be powerful and mark the day that you begin the slow process of letting go and healing from your grief.

Many people who do not have a ceremony or service of any kind report that later on they have regrets and feel incomplete for not doing so. I am a believer that even years later, perhaps on your parent's birthday or the anniversary of their death, you gather with others and have some type of ritual to remember and share stories about your parent(s). Maybe you were too angry at the time of death and simply could not pull something together and now you have experienced forgiveness. The funeral or the celebration of life can mark the beginning of your healing process when it feels positive, supportive, and representative of your mother or father's life.

YOUR PARENT'S BELONGINGS

If this is your last surviving parent who has died you will need to deal with the estate. Hopefully, you and your siblings are getting along well when it comes time to dividing up your parent's possessions and clear plans were laid out regarding who would get what after your parent passed away. Gathering the family to go through items can actually be a very healing and bonding experience. Take the time to reminisce and talk about what certain items meant to you as a child. My mom died nearly ten years ago and I'm still letting go of certain things I just wasn't ready to let go of until now. Don't let others rush you in going through things; do this in your own time. If the items are taking up too much space, or the sale of a home is happening, put things in storage and visit regularly to go through them. You can hire a professional estate liquidator to help you and your family make decisions about what to do. *The Estate Lady,* (Julie Hall, 2007) recommends dividing up what's in your parent's home into these categories:

- Sentimental Value – photographs, jewelry, and your parent's favorite item, such as, your father's guitar or mother's sewing machine. Be aware that everything may feel sentimental.
- Monetary Value – These are items that could be sold for a large sum of money and then divided up between you and your siblings. Get these items professionally appraised.
- Donations – Clothing, furniture, dishes, and appliances are household items that some charities will come and pick up when they are in good condition.
- Recyclables – 50 to 75 percent of what's in a home can be recycled, such as paper, plastic, glass, lumber, and batteries for example.
- Hazardous Materials – Old paint cans, anti-freeze, chemicals, pesticides and cleaning supplies should be disposed of properly.
- Trash – 20 to 25 percent of what is typically in a home is suitable to be thrown away.
- Hall also recommends looking for valuables in odd places. She cautions that older adults are notorious for hiding valuable items in flour, sugar, sewn into clothing or drapes, and even jewelry being placed in toilet tanks.

"What would you attempt to do if you knew you could not fail?"

CHAPTER TEN
Growth And Liberation

"What would you attempt to do if you knew you could not fail?" This question is engraved on a paperweight I received for my fortieth birthday. Still grieving the loss of my dad and now caring for my mom, I mindlessly set it on my desk and didn't really pay attention to it until about eight months after my mom's death. I was feeling a deep sense of losing my purpose. I was no longer a daughter. My role of hyper-vigilance had come to a close. I was in the midst of serious self-reflection and awakening to the fact that I have no control over another's true happiness. While this was a relief and quite freeing for me, I needed to redefine myself and my place in the world.

As I sat at my desk, my eyes caught the words on the paperweight, and I smiled to myself. Suddenly, captivated by it, I picked it up and held it in my hand. I asked myself, "Seriously Karen, what would you attempt to do if you knew you could not fail?" I then searched my heart and mind for a sincere and truthful answer. And then I replied, "If I knew I could not fail, I would go back to school and finish my degree." I attended college for about two years after high school. As the saying goes, "Life is what happens while we're busy making other plans." I never finished my degree, and it haunted me terribly. It was always something nagging at me and never very far away from my surface thoughts. In addition, I had a math phobia and carried a belief in me that I would never be able to pass algebra, especially now, at forty-one years *old. There was evidence in my life that I was intelligent, but this fear always contradicted it, and I felt very ashamed by my perceived failure. I had several vocational certifications; however, this fear prevented me from returning to college to earn a formal degree.*

I made a deal with myself that I would enroll at my local community college and give algebra six months of my undivided attention. If, after that time period I couldn't do it, I would put it to rest and do something else. Prior to enrolling, I purchased CDs to refresh my memory on fractions, division, and prime numbers and so on. I remember taking my first test; I could barely write because my hand was trembling so badly as I struggled to hush the voice in my head that kept telling me I couldn't do it. As the story goes, I was successful in algebra and actually found it to be quite therapeutic for my grieving process, because it gave me a break from my emotions. I got to think and not feel, and it was all about the facts. I decided it was magical and even used it to solve issues I was dealing with in life. For example, isolating the problem and boiling it down until you come up with a solution. Algebra, my adversary for so long, had become my friend. Shockingly, I received one of the highest grades in the class and found myself encouraging much younger students not to give up. I would ask them, "Why do you think I'm here at forty-one-years old?"

I would walk through campus and feel so grateful that I had the space and time in my life to go back to school. My heart felt young again and my life renewed. I would marvel that I wasn't at the hospital or sitting by someone's death bed. I was grateful to be breaking free of my tendency to be a part of someone else's emergency. It took me eight years, but I earned my Associate's, Bachelor's, and Master's degrees and thoroughly enjoyed the process. It was a wonderful gift I gave to myself.

I still miss my parents. If you don't already know this, I will tell you that you don't "get over" someone's death, you adjust to their physical absence. However, sometimes a person leaving allows another to blossom. Because my relationship with both of my parents was so co-dependent, it took them dying for me to be able to own and embrace what is truly important to me in this life. I lived in a state of constant distraction as I tried to make their lives bet-

ter, more fulfilling, and make up for ways I thought I had disappointed them. Some of us just don't truly "grow-up" until our parents die and we're no longer children trying to please them. If this resonates with you, I invite you to tell yourself the truth.

Gather the courage to not simply "pull yourself up by the bootstraps" and carry on with a shielded heart and numbed emotions. Grief potentially cracks our hearts open, and we are offered an opportunity to expand who we are. An open heart offers us many rewards and an enriching and genuine life is one of them. Use the opportunity of grief to grow and know who you truly are. On the other hand, if you had a healthy relationship with your parent(s) and they prepared you well for life, celebrate that and know that as you grieve you will probably take great comfort in sensing that your parent lives on within you. You will be more likely to call on their wisdom or wonder for example, "What would dad do in this situation?" Or, "What would my mom say to resolve this problem?" You will feel inspired to carry on in their honor and memory.

"Hope is an internal awareness that you do not have to suffer forever, and that somehow, somewhere there is a remedy for despair that you will come upon if you can only maintain this expectancy in your heart." Wayne Dyer

---

Whether or not we have a close relationship with our parents, the death of one or both of our parents is a tremendously significant event in our lives. Very often, it is not only an event, but a process that may take weeks, months, or even years. Unless we die first, we all have to confront "losing our parent(s)." If we have enjoyed the company of our parent(s) and they are no longer there, their death can be overwhelming. On the other hand, if we have experienced a difficult relationship or no relationship at all, we may feel an enormous loss and emptiness for what never was and never will be.

"Life shrinks or expands in proportion to one's courage." Anais Nin

---

Wherever you may be in your own personal process, be gentle with yourself and know that there is no right way to grieve or right amount of time it will take to recover and feel like "yourself" again. The truth is, as most people who have been through grieving a death or any major loss, will share, "You're never the same." But, that does not have to be a "bad" thing. When we experience a significant loss, one that triggers our deepest emotions to rise to the surface, we are once again greeted by all other un-resolved losses we have experienced throughout our lives. These emotions invite us to explore that which is deep within us, waiting to be resolved and let go of. The reward is often a sense of profound liberation.

Many people, us wounded warriors, are prone to holding ourselves prisoner to our buried pain. We are bound and shackled by the war of keeping it together; all to maintain control over that which haunts us. When a parent passes away, it can be a powerful time of re-examining your childhood pain and family dynamics. Upon discovering that which truly motivates you and drives your behavior, you may then feel a sense of free-dom to move forward in your life without the burdens you have carried for so many years.

My dad began actively dying, as I recall, at about 9:00 in the morning. I asked my mom, "Why do you have 'The Price is Right' on the TV?" I was re-ally wondering why and how the TV could be on at all. My mom replied, "It's comforting to me, like things are normal." We all respond and cope differently. My brother and I took turns lying next to my dad; we wanted to hold on to every last moment of breath he had. In case he awoke for even a split second, we wanted to be there to grasp and cherish it forever. My mom was terrified as the small world she had known would soon be shrinking even more. As the day continued, she sat next to my dad and thanked him for his love, for their children, for the life they had shared together. It was beautiful, and I was so proud of her courage and strength that day.

It was a beautiful day in April; the sky was blue, the breeze was mild, and white, puffy clouds peppered the sky. At one point, my dad did awaken and kept mumbling, "I love you," over and over again. There we were, the four of us—the original Fazio family-- as I knew it. The four people that had travelled together and overcome so much hardship, so many tears, while still managing to find the humor in life; we were here together, to escort the most cherished of us home. I experienced flashes of us as a family and all we had endured together, all we had overcome. Here we were, thirty-nine years of my life later, at my dad's bedside, just the four of us. Even though my dad was leaving, I had the feeling we made it because he was dying in love, peace, forgiveness, and with dignity. He was dying a quiet death at home, not tragically or suddenly when I was five, ten or fifteen years old. At 3:17 pm on April 17, 2001, he gently exhaled his last breath and left his body behind. At that moment, my watched stopped, as well. It was profound and surreal. Even though I had great relief that he was now on his way home and not suffering, I still could not get my mind around the reality that my dad would no longer be a part of my daily life. And so, the grieving process began.

I had always worried that my mom would die just as soon as my dad did, and I mean literally when I say, "just as soon." She had never lived alone, never really drove a car and had no social life beyond her family. We found her the apartment I mentioned and fortunately, it was near my office. I must say the journey for her was excruciating as she grieved her loss, but she rallied. She enjoyed buying a new sofa that appealed to her, new bedding, and moving to an apartment that was all her own. At times, she reminded me of a young college woman excited to be out on her own for the first time in her life.

I spoke to her on the phone several times a day and visited six days a week. As her COPD progressed, I did the grocery shopping, the laundry, the house-work, took her to the doctor, and did everything I could to buffer the pain of the loss for her. It was not a healthy journey for me, but it was my final chapter as an adult child of alcoholic parents—a co-dependent daughter desperately trying, at the expense of my own right to life, to make the family okay and my mom happy . I had little awareness of where the boundary between us began and ended. In order to heal, I had to consider all of this, but who had time?

"By fully feeling your emotions and expressing the complete truth about them, you will be able to heal the unresolved emotional tension and be free to love more fully" John Gray, PH.D.

My favorite memory of this time is when I would pick her up to go to lunch. The memory still brings tears to my eyes. She would walk down to the front of her apartment building to meet me. I recall my shock each time I would see her all dressed up, smiling, and so excited to spend time with me. It still touches me so deeply because I knew she was hurting so much. Her inner resources absolutely shocked me. The courage, the willingness, and the fight my mom exhibited, left me in awe and taught me to never give up on anyone and don't assume anything.

"WHAT YOU FEEL YOU CAN HEAL"

STAGES OF GRIEF

The five stages of grief: denial, anger, bargaining, depression, and acceptance are a part of the framework that makes up our learning to live with the one we lost. They are tools to help us frame and identify what we may be feeling. But they are not stops on some linear timeline in grief. Not everyone goes through all of them or in a prescribed order. The stages offer us the knowledge of grief's terrain, making us better equipped to cope with life and loss (Elisabeth Kübler-Ross). After your parent dies, try to take some time off from work, reach out to family and friends for support, and if it feels appropriate for you, use some of the holistic modalities named in Chapter Seven to help you begin the healing process. Notice the word *process*. There is no point in time when this experience will not be recognized as a major life event. The process flows like a river with a constant current moving you from one place to the next and perhaps back again. These stages of grief can shift from one to next in a matter of minutes. Please don't interpret these stages as a blueprint for how you should be feeling. I'm including them here as a guide for you to understand how you *may* feel.

DENIAL

Shock, denial, and numbness all help us to survive loss. Over time, the numbness and shock will fade and you will undergo a thawing process, so to speak. In the initial days following a loss, some people cannot think clearly and feel very confused. Others become organizers and are very adept at handling the necessary affairs. There is no "right" way to be.

ANGER

Anger is a necessary stage of the healing process. Be willing to feel your anger, even though it may seem endless. The more you truly feel it, the more it will begin to dissipate, and the more you will heal. There are many other emotions under the anger and you will get to them in time, but anger is the emotion we are most used to managing. The truth is that anger has no limits. It can extend not only to your friends, the doctors, your family, yourself, and your loved one who died, but also to God. You may ask, "Where is God in this?" You may find yourself getting angry with people for saying "stupid things" to you. For example, "Well, your mom was old and lived a long life."

BARGAINING

Before a loss, it seems like you will do anything if only your loved one would be spared. "Please God," you bargain, "I will never be angry at my mom again if you'll just let her live." After a loss, bargaining may take the form of a temporary truce. "What if I devote the rest of my life to helping others? Then can I wake up and realize this has all been a bad dream?" I found myself talking to my dad about possibly trying chemotherapy after all, as if he were still alive.

DEPRESSION

The depressive stage often feels as though it will last forever. It's important to understand that this depression is not a sign of mental illness. It is the appropriate response to a great loss. We withdraw from life, left in a fog of intense sadness. Depression after a loss is too often seen as unnatural: a state to be fixed, something to snap out of. The first question to ask yourself is whether or not the situation you're in is actually depressing. The loss of a loved one is a very depressing situation, and depression is a normal and appropriate response. To not experience depression after a loved one dies would be unusual. When a loss fully settles in your soul, the realization that your loved one didn't get better this time and is not coming back is understandably depressing. If grief is a process of healing, then depression is one of the many necessary steps along the way. Even if you were exhausted from caring for your parent and had initial relief that their suffering was over, you may find yourself wishing you could still care for them.

ACCEPTANCE

This stage is about accepting the reality that our loved one is physically gone and recognizing that this new reality is the permanent reality. We will never like this reality or make it okay, but eventually we accept it. We learn to live with it. It is the new norm with which we must learn to live. We must try to live now in a world where our loved one is missing. In resisting this new norm, many people initially want to maintain life as it was before a loved one died. In time, through bits and pieces of acceptance, we see that we cannot maintain the past intact. It has been forever changed, and we must readjust. We must learn to reorganize roles, reassign them to others, or take them on ourselves. We may start to reach out to others and become involved in their lives. We invest in our friendships and in our relationship with ourselves. We begin to live again, but we cannot do so until we have given grief its time.

(Kübler-Ross)

GRIEF IS PERSONAL

Well-meaning friends and family may try to tell you how to grieve and offer advice on what you *should* do. Be true to yourself and allow yourself to feel what you genuinely are experiencing.   If your parent was very ill over a long period of time, such as in the case of dementia, you may have already grieved by losing them gradually.   It is natural for you to be relieved by their death. You have watched them suffer for many years. You grieved the change in the relationship long ago. Perhaps they did not recognize you for a very long time.   You have known their death was coming for so long; it is now a relief and not something to be anticipated. Some people feel guilty moving on with their lives. They perceive it as a betrayal to the person who has died.   Others are concerned that when their pain fades they will forget their parent. These are natural emotions to have, but bear in mind, the natural course of the grieving process is that you will feel better over time and reengage in life.   Your parent would want this for you. I felt, in the deepest part of my soul, my parent's celebrating my act of enrolling in college again to earn my degree. I called on my dad many times to "assist" me with my algebra journey. As time passes, our parents can become a part of our lives in a different, but a very meaningful way.

WHO AM I NOW?

You may find what I'm about to share disturbing.   However, I am sharing it with the purpose of underscoring the enormity of how grief can "behave." My mom died in the middle of the night. After her body was taken to the mortuary, I tried to get some sleep. Each time I would doze off, I was jolted into the reality that she was gone and in a refrigerator three miles away. I kept having a recurring fear that she wasn't really dead, and I had to get there to care for her. It seemed so sudden; I was caring for her every need, and now she was completely absent, and no one was taking care of her. The "baby monitor" was now turned off, the sucking and thumping sounds of the oxygen compressor had been silenced. My home was eerily quiet, my job was done, my intense purpose over. I was literally beside myself with discomfort. Eventually, these feelings lessoned, but I truly struggled with this thought until after her burial, six days later.

If you were the primary caregiver for your mother or father, don't be surprised if you find yourself feeling lost and without a purpose after your parent dies. No matter your age, losing a parent can be a bewildering experience. Use the time to find new meaning in your life, to reconnect with friends you may not have had time for when you were caregiving. Perhaps your relationship with your spouse or partner suffered while you were caregiving. It may take time to reengage and address issues that are present. If it is possible, take a quiet vacation together that will allow time to talk and be together. If you have become so distanced from one another that this doesn't feel desirable, consider talking to a marriage and family counselor who specializes in grief therapy. It will be imperative for you both to feel understood and validated.

If you have children, remember, they are observing and learning from you how to grieve. Gift your child with a book that speaks to loss and death in an age appropriate manner. They may not only be coping with the loss of a grandparent, but also the emotional loss of you as you cared for your parent and had less time to devote to your family. This is a time of rebuilding and reconnecting with each other so everyone can move forward in a healthy manner.

I FEEL LIKE AN ORPHAN

There is something immensely profound about no longer being someone's child. You may begin to contemplate your own mortality for the first time. You may embark on a goal you had longed to accomplish, but feared your parent's disapproval. You may finally leave the marriage you had wanted to leave for so long, but didn't want to disappoint your parent. Death shakes things loose and people respond, often by rearranging their lives. Family dynamics shift and change. Parents are often the glue that holds family traditions and rituals together. You no longer have your mom or dad filling you in on what your other siblings are doing. You may have to exert more effort to feel connected to your brothers and sisters. Although you may feel disoriented and isolated, it can also be a wonderful time of personal growth for you. You might find yourself reevaluating many things in your life.

SUPPORT GROUPS

Some people find support groups helpful in alleviating the feelings of isolation. Talking and listening to others who are going through a similar experience can be comforting. Hospice organizations and some mortuaries can refer you to a support group. Churches, hospitals, and some community centers offer support groups. Don't be afraid to reach out and find one if you think it will be helpful for you.

OTHER GROUPS AND CLASSES

Consider a meditation, yoga, art, or photography class. Creative activities can help keep you in touch with your true feelings and be very therapeutic and comforting. Some people feel comforted by being in the presence of others, but without expressing their specific challenge. One older friend of mine took great comfort in going to Disneyland by himself after his wife had died. He enjoyed watching the children and others who appeared happy; he felt a part of their happiness.

READING

Reading books on grief can help you to understand what you are experiencing. Even though each person's journey is unique, there are certain sign posts with grief; being aware of these can help you to not feel so alone. There are also some helpful grief workbooks available to help guide you through the process.

EXPLORE YOUR RELATIONSHIP

As I have mentioned, when a parent dies, no matter what your relationship was like, it is an opportunity for growth. Journaling is a powerful way to process your emotions. If you don't want to "ruin" a nice journal with angry or painful words, buy a cheap notebook and write without filtering what you need to express. If you are afraid someone will read it, lock it in a safe or keep it in the truck of your car.

I had an incredible amount of anger for my mom dying angry "after all I had done for her." I always seemed to find myself sitting and reflecting on the fifth step at home. The same step I was sitting on when the mortuary came to pick up her body.

One difficult afternoon while home alone, I burst into uncontrollable tears and expressed every word of anger, sadness, and hurt I had possessed to my mom. It took a long time and I was exhausted afterward. I did this on a regular basis because, as I would express, another layer of pain would reveal itself to me.

About three months later, I was buttering my toast one morning and spontaneously blurted out, "I do love you and forgive you mom." Chills ran through my entire body, and I felt an overpowering sense of love running through me. Was it my mom's presence loving me back? Was the forgiveness I gave releasing me to this loving feeling? Perhaps it doesn't matter what "it" was, except that it was freeing, and I began to feel better in every way. You may also experience little miracles in serendipitous happenings; such as very significant songs playing just when you need it most. For me, more times than I can count and in various settings, I would hear "Dance," various renditions of "Over the Rainbow", and "Ooh Child." The timing of when I would hear these songs was uncanny and brought to me a sense of warmth and hope. Look for and be open to little miracles. If we allow our grieving process to unfold and truly feel the depth of our grief, the disappointments, the pain, and abrasive edges of the relationship we had with our parent(s), are somehow transformed. We let go of the sadness and remember the love. This love is not an illusion or wishful thinking; most likely, it was there all along, yet smothered by the "stuff" of everyday life, past pain, and personal challenges.

NORMAL AND ABNORMAL GRIEF

Again, how a person grieves is unique. In addition, the type of relationship you had with your parent will influence how you grieve. If your parent was abusive to you your entire life, the intensity of your grief may be diminished. If your parent was ill for many, many years, it would be natural for you to feel relieved. Having sadness, tears and low energy is normal; however, if you are spending all day in bed and not able to function in your daily life after a couple of months, you should reach out for professional help. While it's important to "feel to heal," if depression is severe, you may need to take medication for a while to help you function and alleviate your suffering. If you have insomnia for an extended period of time, you may also want to consider medication for the short term (Hogan, 2010). Make an appointment with your physician to discuss your depression and they can give you the appropriate referral, if necessary. Reaching out for "holistic" (Chapter Seven modalities) assistance early in your process may help prevent severe depression and crippling anxiety; thereby helping you to avoid the necessity of taking medication.

HOLIDAYS, BIRTHDAYS, AND ANNIVERSARIES

Expect that holidays and anniversaries, especially the first ones, may trigger your grief again. You may be reminded of how much you miss your mother or father, or both. You may reflect excessively about how things used to be, how things are just not the same, and how your family has changed. You may feel sad and tearful. Don't hesitate to journal about how you feel. Have lunch with a good friend and talk about it. Reach out to family members and inquire about how they are feeling. Find a way to honor your parent. Taking flowers to the cemetery is sometimes helpful. Sitting in nature and reflecting can be a good idea. Consider planning a family dinner in your mother and/or father's memory and share stories.

A NEW NORMAL

As time passes the intensity of your grief will fade, you will gradually resume normal activities, and reengage in important relationships. You may become interested in taking on a new profession or project or change jobs altogether. You may have gained a new perspective on life and how you want to live yours. Life may now feel more meaningful to you or you may feel inspired to not make the same "mistakes" your parent made.

The good memories of your parent may become more dominant in your thoughts, rather than the sadness and pain. You may find yourself focusing more on your parent's positive personality traits and embrace the presence of them within you.

Over time, your family will create new holiday and birthday traditions that will feel good to you. You may find it to be a wonderful time to share memories of your parents or use your mother's recipe for the family's favorite dish. Each Christmas my mom and dad would give me a beautiful wall calendar and my mom would write on my birthday, "Happy Birthday Dear, we love you!" I ached each Christmas when I didn't get that calendar after my parents had passed. After three years, I began buying my own calendar and writing "Happy Birthday" on it myself. Hold on to the hope that as you go forward with courage a new normal will develop and you will adjust to the changes in your life.

"Each day, intend to become the person you had always hoped to be." K. Fazio

AFTERWORD
A New Understanding

As you review and examine the relationship you had with your parent(s), your perspective of history may change. As I forgave my mom, it seemed as if I gained access to an understanding so deep and genuine that I have no adequate words to give the experiences justice. I can only equate it to staring at a jigsaw puzzle for many, many years with the ability to place a piece here and there, but never being able to bring into view the complete picture. You try a piece here and there, but it doesn't fit. For me, I was able to link my mom and dad's childhood stories and early adulthood experiences and losses to why our relationship developed in the way it did.

My heart opened more and more and I gained a deep empathy for my parents. I put the pieces together of why my parents had so much unresolved grief. My heart opened wide in compassion for my mom as I recalled the story of her traumatic birth and being left for dead in a sink until a heroic nurse took her out to revive her. I came to understand my mom's deep frustration in never becoming who she wanted to be and how my dad, unknowingly fostered this repression. In addition, I gained insight and acknowledged the personality traits I have in common with my parents. I'm not trying to say that "I'm practically perfect in every way" since my parents died. What I am saying is that I feel liberated and free to live the life that is authentic for me, not the life my parent's had crafted for me in their own minds. I feel the freedom to "unfold" in a genuine way; a freedom I don't believe I could have experienced with my parents physically present.

After my parents died, I was able to truly see and understand how my patterns of co-dependence were driving my life and the way in which I would go about making decisions. I had the opportunity to grieve many losses and unmet needs. I came to realize and relinquish my motivations for constantly trying to make up for what I perceived as insufficiencies in myself.

You may find some wonderful surprises during your journey; look for signs. During my mom's last month of life, I would leave early in the morning for a run. I would leave a note at her bedside telling her when I would return and always write, "I love you." I found one of my notes tucked away in a drawer about six months after my mom had died. She had written next to my "I love you," "I love you too, so much." I inherited my mom's sewing cabinet. In the cabinet is a small box filled with safety pins. When I was a child, I frequently would go to this little cardboard box to get a safety pin. One day at home, about a year after my mom had died, the string slipped through a pair of my sweatpants. I went to the little box to get a safety pin to feed the string back through. On the underside of the top of the box I found a note my mom had written to me, "I love and miss you so much." These two occasions, and others like them, were profoundly freeing and healing for me.

The timing of when I found items seemed to be directly correlated to where I was in my grieving process. If you have had a difficult relationship with one or both of your parents, don't assume it's too late to resolve things because they have died.

Forgiveness frees the heart to live and to love, but first you have to be honest with yourself about what you are angry and hurt about. This deep and sincere honesty will reveal things to you about yourself that were previously hidden away. When we do this, it's as if the pain naturally transforms itself into forgiveness, for others as well as for ourselves. I also found myself lighting a candle, quieting myself and asking my parents for their forgiveness for the unkind words I had spoken to them, as well as for any pain I had unknowingly inflicted upon them.

When my dad died I was thirty-nine-years-old. I was forty-one-years-old when my mom passed away, and I began writing this book just before my fiftieth birthday. *Caring, grieving, and growing* indeed, is an ongoing journey which hopefully leads us to our highest and deepest truth. It is then, that we are able to live our lives, motivated and inspired by this meaningful truth - offering the world our most genuine and loving selves.

RESOURCES

Aging With Dignity
Download Health Directive- "Five Wishes"
www.agingwithdignity/five-wishes.org

Amyotrophic Lateral Sclerosis (ALS) Association
www.alsa.org

Alzheimer's Association
alz.org

American Association of Retired Persons (AARP)
www.aarp.org

American Cancer Society
www.cancer.org

American Diabetes Association
www.diabetes.org

American Heart Association
www.americanheart.org

American Holistic Association
www.ahha.org

American Massage Therapy Association
www.amtamassage.org

American Stroke Association
www.strokeassociation.org

Area Agency on Aging-Check for Local Office

Braille Institute of America
www.brailllibrary.org

Driving Tips for Seniors/Concerns
www.helpguide.org/elder

Eden Alternative (For Person Directed Care)
www.edenalt.org

Eldercare Locator
A public service of the U.S. Administration on Aging; will connect you to
a variety of services for older adults.
www.eldercarelocator.gov

Eldercare Mediators
www.eldercaremediators.com

Hoarding Task Force
Check for a resource in your parent's area

Home Safety Checklist
Download AT:
www.rebuildingtogether.org

Lung Disease
www.lungusa.org

Medicaid
http://medicaid.gov

Medi-cal
www.medi-cal.ca.gov

Medicare
www.medicare.gov

National Alliance for Caregiving
Publications and resources for caregivers, including the Famly Care Resource Connection, where you can find reviews and ratings of more than 1,000 books, videos, websites, and other materials on caregiving.
www.caregiving.org

National Association of Geriatric Care Managers
www.caremanager.org

National Association of People With Aids
www.napwa.org

National family Caregivers Association
Educational materials for family caregivers
www.thefamilycaregiver.org/caregiving_resources

Nursing Home Comparison
www.medicare.gov/nhcompare.org

Ombudsman
www.eldercarelocator.org
Also, check your Area Agency on Aging
Orange County, CA: www.coaoc.org

Prepare To care
A Planning Guide for Families
www.aarp.org

Senior Action in a Gay Environment (SAGE)
www.sageusa.org

Seniors and the Affordable Care Act
www.healthcare.gov

SMP: Empowering Seniors To Prevent Medicare Fraud
www.smpresource.org

State Health Insurance Counseling and Assistance Programs (SHIPs)
SHIP programs go by different names in each state. Contact the Area
Agency on Aging near your parent(s).
Orange County, CA www.coaoc.org

Veterans Administration
www.va.gov

RECOMMENDED READING

Caregiving

Boomer Burden
Julie Hall – "The Estate Lady"

Coping With Your Difficult Older Parent
Grace Lebow & Barbara Kane

Coping with Dementia: What Every Caregiver Needs to Know
Rosemary De Cuir

How To Care For Aging Parents
Virginia Morris

Navigating The Journey Of Aging Parents – What Care Receivers Want
Cheryl A. Kuba

Stages of Senior Care
Paul and Lori Hogan

Holistic Care and Self-Help
Empowerment through Reiki
Paula Horan

Feel The Fear And Do It Anyway
Susan Jeffers

The Disease To Please: Curing the People-Pleasing Syndrome
Harriet B. Braiker

Co-dependent No More
Melody Beattie

There's A Spiritual Solution To Every Problem
Wayne W. Dyer

The Gift Of Change: Spiritual Guidance for a Radically New Life
Marianne Williamson

The Heart of the Buddha's Teachings: Transforming Suffering into Peace,
joy, and Liberation
Thich Nhat Hanh

Stillness Speaks
Eckhart Tolle

End of Life and Grief
Living With Death And Dying
Elisabeth Kübler-Ross

Losing A Parent
Alexandra Kennedy

Tuesdays with Morrie
Mitch Albom

INDEX

AARP 69, 148, Resources

Acceptance 75, 84, 132, 134

Active, aging 2, 81, 100

Activities Of Daily Living 5, 11, 28, 87

Acupuncture 80, 82, 88

Adult Day Care 11, 62

Advanced Directive 21, 22, 27

Agency, homecare 28, 34, 43, 48, 49, 55, 56, 59

Aging 17, 27, 28, 33, 34, 43, 51, 55, 61, 81, 82, 90, 99, 100, 103

Aging In Place 28, 55, 61

Alzheimer's Disease, association 8, 46, 62

Anxiety 70, 71, 84, 88, 91, 92, 139

Assessment 6, 50, 60

Assisted Living Facility 10, 22, 44, 71, 101, 103, 114

Attorney 12, 17, 19, 20, 27

Bach Flower Remedies 80, 91-92

Burnout, caregiver 31, 56, 68-75

Bathroom, safety 6, 60, 61, 100, 101

Belongings, parent's 18, 54, 123

Caregiver, bill of rights 75

Caregiver, burnout 31, 68

Caregiving, family 3, 5, 75, 98, 99, 147

Caregiving, general 2, 6, 8, 10, 21, 90, 95, 105, 115, 136, 147, 148

Caregiver, professional 5, 22, 99

Cataracts 7

Ceremony, importance of 121, 123

Changes, health 55, 60, 69, 83

Changes, housing 6, 55, 61

Changes, mood, personality, relationships 8, 9, 42, 80, 118, 140

Children, adult 3, 7, 22, 27, 30, 33, 34, 43, 44, 47, 48, 50, 61, 65, 105

Children, impact on 42, 67, 136

Classes, for families 45, 62

Classes, for seniors 26, 87, 90, 100, 137

Co-dependence, caregiving and 38, 73, 142

Cognitive, decline, function 8, 9, 59, 60, 99

Communication, healthy 21, 39, 40, 41, 51, 90,

Complementary and Alternative Medicine 81

Conflict, family 18, 45, 46, 49, 50, 51

Continuum of Care Retirement Community (CCRC) 100

Conversations, dying process 112, 119

Conversations, important 106, 21, 24, 27

Coping 12, 45, 94, 136

Cost, care 62, 99

Costs, living, housing 24, 99-103, 123

Counseling 43, 48, 50, 76

Cremation 23, 111, 121, 122

Death 90, 94, 109-124

Dementia 4, 7, 8, 90, 99, 101, 103, 135

Dementia, coping with 45, 55, 62, 71

Depression 3, 7, 8, 9, 10, 33, 46, 59, 70, 84-88, 90-93, 132, 134, 139

Diabetes 8, 145

Difficult, relationships, people 21, 33, 47, 49, 130, 142, 149

Documents, important 11, 17-28

Driving, safety 6, 8, 10, 22, 25-26, 146

Eden Alternative 104, 146

Elder Law Attorney 18

Eldercare Locator 146

Emotions, difficult 4, 10, 39, 48-50, 71, 76-85, 90-92, 105, 129, 130-137

End-Of-Life 19, 23, 80, 111, 116, 151

Estate, parent's 17-20, 123-124

Eyesight 7

Exercise 63, 75, 90-95

Faith 76, 94, 114

Falls, prevention 5-, 8, 61, 90

Fear 5, 51, 109, 135

Finances 11, 18-21, 28

Fraud 148

Funerals 111

Future, planning for 3, 11, 59, 90

Geriatric Care Manager 27-28, 45, 50, 147

Grief 54-56, 80, 90, 98, 109-151

Guided Autobiography 91

Guided Imagery 91

Guilt, feelings of 23, 33, 42, 48-50, 74-76, 84, 92-98, 105, 116, 121, 135

Healthy, caregiving practices 61-63, 68, 72, 75, 81-95, 99, 136

Healthcare, decisions 113

Health, decline 3, 5, 7, 11, 17, 19, 24-34, 41-51

Health, promotion 104

Hearing, loss 7, 11, 51, 60

Hiring, caregiver 5, 28, 33, 55-59, 98

Hobbies 93

Holidays 9, 105, 139

Holistic, care, modalities 23, 81-93, 132, 146

Home Modification/Monitoring 60-61

Hospice and Palliative Care 23, 42, 54, 58, 66, 103, 111, 112-115, 119-137

Hospital 19, 72, 111, 121, 137

Housing, options 6, 19, 22, 100

Insurance 11, 20, 40, 56, 113, 148

Journaling 93-95, 137

LGBT, family member, you 46-47

Lighting 60, 89

Listening 16, 44, 137

Living Options 99-106

Long-Distance Caregiving 9, 27, 34, 39, 41, 44

Long-term Care, facilities 104-106

Long-term Care, policies 20, 56

Massage 76, 86, 146

Massage, geriatric 80-83, 87

Medicaid 20, 56, 103, 147

Medi-CAL 56, 147

Medicare 11, 20, 103, 113, 147

Medication Management 6-9, 20, 28, 32, 45, 50-55, 60, 63, 102, 118

Meditation 80-, 89, 115, 137

Memory Care 8-9, 46, 101-102

Mental Illness 49, 134

Mobility 9, 60, 87, 89

Moods, changes, swings 94, 118

Non-Medical, caregiving 11, 55

Nutrition 74, 93-95

Ombudsman 106, 148

Oral Care 7, 11, 51

Orphan, feel like 136

Pain, emotional, physical 9, 48, 50, 54, 70, 79, 82, 87-99, 105, 130-133

Physical, care, issues 3, 10, 11, 34, 45, 50, 51, 63, 69-70, 80-95

Physical Therapy 63, 87-89

Placement, emotions of, time for 97-99, 105

Placement Specialist 104-105

Planning, for care 3, 17, 27, 105

Prayer 82, 89-90-94

Psychotherapy 86, 90

Reading 9, 93-94, 137, 149

Reiki 80, 82, 86, 92, 150

Relationships 9, 32, 40-43, 93, 139

Religion 85, 92, 114-115

Retirement 9, 18, 97, 100

Senior Centers 82

Sibling, relationships 27, 34, 40-49, 71, 86, 106, 123-124, 136

Skilled Nursing 100, 103, 106

Sleep Hygiene, importance of 92

Spirituality 85, 114

Stress, management/prevention 65-72, 92-94

Support, groups/classes 10, 12, 22, 33-34, 42-50, 87, 101, 113, 132, 137

Support, Alzheimer's Association 62

Tai Chi 90

Taxes 18, 56

Terminal Restlessness 118

Tools, for coping, survival,
    empowerment 75, 82, 86, 94, 132

Touch, importance of 80, 86

Training, professional caregivers
    57, 101

Universal Design 61

Vision 61

Wills 18, 27

Zen, caregiving 79-95

Made in United States
Orlando, FL
05 February 2024

43343387R00098